BJ
2051
.W26
1996

BEVERL

W9-DGG-378

The Best

Wedding

Ever

DISCARD

By
Diane Warner

CHICAGO PUBLIC LIBRARY
BEVERLY BRANCH
1962 W. 95th STREET
CHICAGO, IL   60643

CAREER PRESS
3 Tice Road
P.O. Box 687
Franklin Lakes, NJ 07417
1-800-CAREER-1
201-848-0310 (NJ and outside U.S.)
FAX: 201-848-1727

Copyright © 1996 by Diane Warner

All rights reserved under the Pan-American and International Copyright Conventions. This book may not be reproduced, in whole or in part, in any form or by any means electronic or mechanical, including photocopying, recording, or by any information storage and retrieval system now known or hereafter invented, without written permission from the publisher, The Career Press.

Note: Due to the constantly changing nature of the wedding industry, neither the author nor the publisher make any guarantees as to the availability or costs of features described in this book.

THE BEST WEDDING EVER
ISBN 1-56414-236-1, $11.99
Cover design by Dean Johnson Design, Inc.
Cover photo by Telegraph Color Library/FPG International
Printed in the U.S.A. by Book-mart Press

To order this title by mail, please include price as noted above, $2.50 handling per order, and $1.00 for each book ordered. Send to: Career Press, Inc., 3 Tice Road, P.O. Box 687, Franklin Lakes, NJ 07417.

Or call toll-free 1-800-CAREER-1 (NJ and Canada: 201-848-0310) to order using VISA or MasterCard, or for further information on books from Career Press.

Library of Congress Cataloging-in-Publication Data

Warner, Diane.
    The best wedding ever / by Diane Warner.
       p.   cm.
    Includes index.
    ISBN 1-56414-236-1 (pbk.)
    1. Wedding etiquette.   I. Title.
BJ2051.W26   1996
395'.22--dc20   96-15773
                                                                                CIP

Other wedding books by Diane Warner

How to Have a Big Wedding on a Small Budget

*Big Wedding on a Small Budget
Planner and Organizer*

*Beautiful Wedding Decorations and
Gifts on a Small Budget*

*How to Have a Fabulous, Romantic
Honeymoon on a Budget*

Complete Book of Wedding Vows

CHICAGO PUBLIC LIBRARY
BEVERLY BRANCH
1962 W. 95th STREET
CHICAGO, IL   60643

Dedication

With love to my grandson, Caleb.

CHICAGO PUBLIC LIBRARY
BEVERLY BRANCH
2121 W 95TH ST   60643

Acknowledgments

My thanks go to all of you who supplied me with such challenging questions, to those wedding professionals who contributed toward the accuracy of my answers and, most especially, to all those brides and grooms who so generously opened their hearts to share their own ideas and experiences with you, my readers, so that you may have "the best wedding ever."

CHICAGO PUBLIC LIBRARY
BEVERLY BRANCH
1962 W. 95th STREET
CHICAGO, IL   60643

Contents

Introduction: Did You Know That I Love You?   11

Chapter 1: The Engagement Period   13

Chapter 2: Wedding Jewelry   17

Chapter 3: Planning a Wedding   25

Chapter 4: The Bridal Registry   39

Chapter 5: Who Pays for What?   45

Chapter 6: Inviting the Guests   51

Chapter 7: The Bride   61

Chapter 8: The Groom   73

Chapter 9: The Bride's Attendants   79

Chapter 10: The Groom's Attendants   83

Chapter 11: The Couple's Parents   85

Chapter 12: Themes and Decorations   89

Chapter 13: The Rehearsal   95

Chapter 14: The Ceremony   99

Chapter 15: The Reception   111

Chapter 16: Photography and Videography   135

Chapter 17: The Flowers   147

Chapter 18: The Music   153

Chapter 19: The Transportation   159

Chapter 20: All Those Extras   163

Chapter 21: The Honeymoon   173

Epilogue   185

Index   187

Did You Know That I Love You?

Well, I do! You see, after writing six wedding-related books and conducting countless wedding seminars, I have developed a real love and compassion for all of you brides and grooms out there who are trying to plan the most important day of your lives. Although I've never met you personally, I feel as if I know you. I empathize with you as you struggle with the decisions that must be made, from your engagement ring to your reception theme to your honeymoon plans. I know you have hundreds of questions and I hope you'll find the answers here. God bless you as you plan. This book has been written with my sincere love and best wishes that you will have *the best wedding ever.*

Your friend,

Diane Warner

Chapter 1

The Engagement Period

How does an engagement party differ from a shower? Are gifts expected?

An *engagement party* is a party given in honor of the newly engaged couple; it may be formal or informal. Often, when it is hosted by the bride's parents, it is a formal sit-down dinner where the couple is toasted and lavished with love and congratulations on their engagement. Gifts may or may not be given at this type of formal occasion, but if they are, they are often family heirlooms that are being passed down. Or it can be a very informal party hosted by peers of the couple, and gifts may or may not be given in this case as well; however, if gifts are part of the celebration, the party usually becomes more of a co-ed *shower*.

Should my parents be expected to host an engagement party even though my fiance and I are paying for the entire wedding?

They aren't necessarily *expected* to host this celebration, but they should be asked if they would like to, since the bride's parents usually host the first engagement party. After they have had the opportunity, anyone may play host, including the groom's parents; having two or more engagement parties is not uncommon. By the way, if money is a problem, this doesn't have to be an expensive affair—ice cream sundaes on the patio are fine!

How should we word our engagement announcement for our local newspaper? And how soon should we send it in?

Call the newspaper to find out what they require as far as advance notice of your announcement; although the announcement usually appears a month or so before the wedding, many society editors need the submission a month earlier than that so it can be scheduled. As far as the wording goes, the best reference is your local newspaper itself. Save the engagement announcements over a few months' time and use the wording to help you compose your own unique announcement.

Some society editors write the announcements themselves and will ask you for the following:

- Names and addresses of the bride and groom.
- Names and address of the bride's parents.
- Names of the bride's grandparents.
- Date, time and place of the ceremony.
- Names of the attendants.
- Descriptions of the wedding attire to be worn by the bride and her attendants.
- The bride's and groom's educational background and professions.
- Where the couple will be honeymooning.
- Where the couple will be residing after the honeymoon.

What is an "announcement party"?

An announcement party is similar to an engagement party except that the engagement is formally announced for the first time during this party. It is usually attended by relatives and close friends, may be formal or informal and is often a surprise announcement, although everyone probably suspected as much, having seen that love light in your eyes. By the way, this is usually the first time the bride wears her engagement ring.

What is the ideal length of an engagement?

Although the average length of an engagement today is 15 months, I personally favor a shorter engagement period. Once you've found each other, it's very difficult to wait so long to get married; however, it isn't uncommon these days for a wedding date to be set 12 to 18 months in advance to allow time for booking the sites, the caterer, photographer, etc.

What if a couple becomes engaged long before the groom can afford an engagement ring?

Then, become engaged and make the formal announcements—no problem. It doesn't take a ring to seal the commitment! In fact, I've known of dozens of couples who have put off the engagement ring until the first or second wedding anniversary, marrying in a simple double-ring ceremony.

What's the best advice you can give us during our engagement period?

My best advice is this: Try to relax and bask in this magical, Cinderella time of your lives. Don't let the wedding plans work you into a lather of anxiety—it's just not worth it!

Chapter 2

Wedding Jewelry

Does an engagement ring have to be a diamond ring to be "official"?

Although diamond rings are the most popular (75 percent of the women who will marry this year are wearing a diamond), there are many other gems that are equally as beautiful and "official," including a ruby, sapphire, emerald, amethyst or pearl. In fact, any birthstone may be placed in a setting of your choice and worn as an engagement ring. Another popular custom is to convert an heirloom ring into an engagement ring by providing a modern setting for the stone (average cost about $900).

How did the tradition of wearing a diamond ring as an engagement ring start?

The idea of the engagement ring itself came from the ancient belief that a bride-to-be should wear a ring on the third finger of her left hand because it was thought that this finger was the only one with a vein that ran directly to the heart. The tradition of the diamond also came from an ancient belief that its sparkle was a "flame of love."

What is the average size of a diamond in an engagement ring in the United States?

According to a recent survey published in *USA Today*, the average size of an engagement diamond is .75 carat.

I've heard that many couples set up a joint bank account to pay for everything, including the wedding and honeymoon. Can the rings be paid for out of this account, too?

You're right. It has become quite common these days for the couple themselves to share all the expenses, with this one exception: The groom usually pays for the bride's engagement and wedding rings, and the bride usually pays for the groom's wedding ring, if he is to wear one.

How can I find an honest, reputable jeweler?

Try to find one who has been in business a long time, is recommended by your friends and, preferably, is a member of the *American Gem Society*, a professional organization that prides itself on its high ethical standards. Avoid the jeweler who advertises that he *only* carries "flawless" or "blue white" diamonds; these gems are so rare that jewelers usually do not carry more than a few of them. Also, be suspicious of any jeweler who says he sells "wholesale to the public" because his wholesale price may actually be higher than another jeweler's retail price. Once you've selected an engagement ring, make the sale contingent on an *independent* appraisal, which you will have to pay for yourself, but which will give you peace of mind that the stone is as represented. If the jeweler won't let you have the ring appraised by an independent appraiser, take this as a red flag and walk away from the deal!

What is this I keep hearing about the "two-month" rule when purchasing an engagement ring?

This rule of thumb was conveniently calculated by diamond merchants and jewelers who would like you to spend two months' salary on the ring. Don't take this too seriously, and please don't feel guilty if you can't meet their imposed standard. Spend only what you can afford, and remember, you can always add a diamond or purchase a more expensive setting as an anniversary gift some day when your income is higher and you don't have so many other expenses.

Our wedding rings didn't come cheap; do we dare entrust them to our 4-year-old ring bearer, even though they will be tied onto the pillow with ribbons?

I think for your peace of mind it would be best to let the ring bearer carry inexpensive fakes. The best man and the bride's honored attendant should be the caretakers of the actual wedding rings.

What are the "four Cs"?

They are the four qualities that determine a diamond's value: *cut, clarity, color* and *carat*. Before you purchase a diamond engagement ring you should know these four Cs by heart; when you walk into a jewelry store, be as knowledgeable as possible. *Cut* refers to the shape of the diamond; *clarity* is ranked on a scale from "F1" (flawless) to "F13" (imperfect); *color* is ranked on a scale from "D" (colorless) to "Y" (yellow); and *carat* indicates the weight of the diamond. Jewelers will start out with a display of flawless, colorless one-carat diamonds, and, of course, that's what you'll want to purchase. However, the price tag could run as high as 12 months' salary, so try to keep your head. *The more you spend doesn't mean the more you love her.* Don't let anyone put you on this guilt trip!

Are the four Cs visible to the naked eye?

A diamond's size, measured in carats, is obvious to the naked eye, of course, as is the diamond's cut, which is the number and shape of the facets. When light reflects off the facets of a diamond, there should be a brilliance of constantly changing colors and intensities. The cut should "knock your eyes out," in other words. The other Cs, clarity and color, are more subtle qualities. In fact, it is said that the true clarity and color of a diamond can only be seen when the diamond is magnified tenfold, and how many times is that likely to happen? The clarity is what you see or don't see deep inside the magnified diamond. There are very few flawless diamonds; most have small areas that look like tiny crystals or air bubbles when seen through a jeweler's eyeglass.

Finally, when it comes to color, a diamond may be blue, yellow, brown or even black, but the less color it has, the more valuable it is. It is said that colorless diamonds are as rare as flawless diamonds, but, like clarity, color is very difficult for the layman to detect. So, we're back to the two visible qualities: carat (size) and cut. Most of the women I've talked to say they would much rather have a large diamond that has a few "invisible" flaws than a smaller one that is closer to perfect, which brings me to an interesting experience I had recently. A jeweler displayed to me two diamond solitaire rings, each priced at $5,000. The one diamond, half-carat in size, was clear and flawless; the other was a carat and a half of lesser quality. He said the only way the average person could tell the difference between the quality of the two diamonds was to lay them side by side, and when he did, I could see that the smaller diamond had more of a clear, "see-through," blue quality, while the larger diamond didn't have quite as much sparkle and had a very slight yellow cast. However, when the larger diamond was separated from the smaller and worn out in the sunlight, it looked awfully darned good!

What does the jeweler mean by the term "setting"?

The setting is simply the design of the ring, the way the stones are arranged within the metal of the ring itself. For example, a Tiffany setting, which is a traditional solitaire setting, perches a single diamond high on the band, to "show it off." An Illusion setting is one that contains several stones, usually a group of smaller stones surrounding a larger one. There are thousands of settings to choose from, some delicate and lacy, others simple and elegant.

What about our wedding bands? What's the difference between 14 karat and 24 karat, for example?

If you're talking about gold bands, they usually range from 10 to 24 karat, depending on how pure they are. Twenty-four karat is so pure that it's actually quite soft and might wear or bend easily. Fourteen karat is the most common. The karat numbers reflect how many parts gold and how many parts of another metal. For example, 24-karat gold is 24 parts gold; 18-karat gold is 18 parts gold and six parts of another metal, and so on. Wedding bands also come in platinum which is extremely durable and doesn't wear away as easily as gold.

Do most couples have their wedding rings engraved?

Yes, most do. Usually they have their initials engraved, along with the date of the wedding. For example, "E.L.K. to B.J.M. 10-3-96." You can include anything you would like, of course, as long as it fits inside your ring. Sometimes couples have references to Bible verses engraved in their rings, such as: *"Mt. 19:6"* which would be a reference to Matthew 19:6: *"Whatsoever God hath joined together, let no man put asunder."* You may also select a line from a favorite romantic poem or love song. A recent *Washington Post Magazine* article tells about a couple who had their rings inscribed with this line of poetry: *"I send you a cream-white rosebud,"* a line from a poem titled "A White Rose" by the Irish-American poet John Boyle O'Reilly that says: "I send you a cream-white rosebud...for the love that is purest and sweetest." There are other more traditional ring engravings, as well, such as these: "I will be yours while life endures," "In thee my choice do I rejoice" and "God for me appointed thee."

Doesn't the wedding band have to match the engagement ring? Why do some couples wait until the last minute to buy their wedding bands?

The bride's wedding band usually matches her engagement ring and is purchased as a set; however, the band may also be selected at a later date. As far as waiting until the last minute to buy the bands, that isn't uncommon, although the ring has usually been selected ahead of time or even put on layaway. If it's a double-ring ceremony, the bride usually chooses a wedding band for her groom that is well-matched to her own, except that it will be a little heavier.

What happens in the unfortunate chance that a wedding is called off? Is the woman obligated to return the engagement ring to her fiance?
Yes.

What should I wear in the way of jewelry on my wedding day? My wedding gown has a sweetheart neckline.
The thing to remember here is that *less is better*. Don't load up on flashy jewelry, especially colored gems or stones; keep it simple. A single strand of pearls, pearl earrings and your engagement ring, worn on your right hand, of course, would be just right. In any case, never wear your watch during the ceremony.

Sometimes I see wedding rings worn on the right hand instead of the left. Why is this?
Many couples wear their wedding rings on the fourth finger of the right hand, depending on their religious or ethnic heritage. It is common in Germany, for example, for the man and woman to wear gold rings on the fourth finger of their left hands when they become engaged, transferring them to their right hands during the wedding ceremony. It's interesting that in Southern Germany an engagement is considered so binding that the couple are known as "bridegroom" and "bride" beginning on the first day the gold rings are placed on their left hands.

My fiancee's divorce isn't final yet, but she hasn't worn her wedding ring for almost a year. I've bought her an engagement ring; is it all right for her to wear it now?

I know that in your minds she is already divorced from her first husband and committed to you. However, legally she is still someone else's wife, so she shouldn't wear your engagement ring until the day the divorce is final.

What if the rings won't slide onto our fingers during the ceremony?

This is a pretty common occurrence, actually, because even though the rings fit just fine before the ceremony, stress can cause fingers to swell and when you try to slide the ring over the knuckle, it gets stuck. If this should happen, here are a couple easy solutions: either slide it on as far as it will go without forcing it (then casually slide it the rest of the way as you walk down the aisle during the recessional), or slide it onto the pinky finger until after the ceremony (none of the guests will notice) and then use a little salad oil, hand lotion or petroleum jelly to ease it onto the proper finger. Whatever happens, don't panic! It's not worth it, believe me. You'll be just as married whether the ring fits or not.

Chapter 3

Planning a Wedding

What are some of the latest wedding trends in this country?

Here are several for you to consider in your planning:

- A move away from Cinderella "fluff" to sophisticated elegance (not only for the ceremony and reception themes, but the bridal attire, as well).
- Because wedding costs are so high, there is more sharing of the total expense, not only by both sets of parents, but by the couple themselves. In fact, the couple, especially a professional couple who have been living on their own for a number of years, often pay for the entire wedding.
- Destination weddings (getting married at your honeymoon destination).
- More candid photography shots than ever.
- Donating leftover reception food to food kitchens for the poor.
- Multiflavored wedding cakes.
- No more plastic bride and groom cake toppers— more creative alternatives instead.
- Food stations at the reception (see Chapter 15) and cappuccino and espresso bars in place of alcoholic beverages.

- Using interesting alternatives to the standard limo (see Chapter 19).
- Cummerbunds and bow ties made out of the same fabric as the bridesmaids' dresses.
- Fewer pastels and more deep, intense colors, such as hunter green, deep burgundy, navy blue and black.
- Couples writing their own vows.
- Children from previous marriages being incorporated into the ceremony.
- Couples facing the congregation during the ceremony (as opposed to having their backs to them).
- Older brides (in 1950 the average bride was 18; in 1990, the average age of first-time brides was 24).
- Doing away with receiving lines.
- A designated, supervised "play room" for any children in attendance (where they can watch videos, color and play games).
- More DJs and fewer bands at receptions.
- Incorporation of the couple's ethnic backgrounds into the wedding's theme.
- More buffets; fewer sit-down dinners.
- Fewer aisle runners.

We just became engaged and we're overwhelmed with all the things we need to plan. Where should we start?

The first thing you need to do is decide what type of service you want; all your other plans will hinge on this one important decision. By *type of service* I mean whether it will be traditional or nontraditional, religious or civil, one faith or interfaith. Don't let your engagement euphoria rob you of some calm "dreaming time." You need to close your eyes and try to envision your wedding. What do you see? A vast cathedral with stained glass windows? A small ivy-covered brick chapel? Or a wedding on a hillside overlooking a sandy beach? Once you have this settled in your mind, all the other plans will come naturally, including the wedding date, style of bridal gown, number of attendants and guests, flowers, music and theme decorations. I know you feel like hummingbirds with no place to sit, but find an empty branch and alight long enough to make this first weighty decision.

What months are considered the slow months for weddings, when everything might be less expensive?

Usually, November through January.

What is the most expensive day of the week to get married?

Saturday, and more specifically, Saturday at 7 p.m.

What about the time of day for the wedding? Are there certain traditions about that?

The traditions have mainly to do with restrictions due to the couple's religious faith. For example, a Jewish wedding is traditionally held after sundown on a Saturday evening or on a Sunday; it may never be held on the Sabbath (between sundown on a Friday and sundown on a Saturday.) Also, most Roman Catholic weddings are held between eight in the morning and noon, although that custom has been relaxed quite a bit in the past 20 years or so. One of the first things you need to do is meet with your clergyman to clear the date and time of your wedding.

What determines the formality of a wedding?

There are three basic degrees of formality: *formal, semiformal* and *informal*. The degree is related to the elegance and formality of the ceremony and reception sites, the size of the wedding party and the number of guests. A wedding with more than 200 guests would usually be considered *formal*; 75 to 200 would be considered *semiformal*; and less than 75, *informal*. Then there are other rules of thumb. For example, a home wedding is usually considered to be *informal*. Once the degree of formality is established, it should be consistent with the type of invitations selected, the length and style of the bridal gown, the men's attire, the type of food served at the reception and the amount and elegance of the flowers. These variations are discussed, by the way, in the following chapters.

Do you happen to know what percentage of brides today choose a formal wedding?

Yes, and I have it broken down by ages, as well:

- Age 18 to 25: 51 percent
- Age 26 to 35: 33 percent
- Age 36 and up: 14 percent

Obviously, the older the bride, the more informal the wedding.

Although they may not actually consider themselves to be "religious," I've heard that many couples want a religious ceremony in a church or synagogue. Do you have any statistics on this?

The latest figures show that approximately 75 percent of all marriages today are considered to be religious and are held in some type of religious establishment.

My father is deceased; who shall I ask to give me away at my wedding?

Very often, due to divorce, death or illness, a bride is given away by someone else. You may ask another male relative or family friend to escort you down the aisle, or you may choose to walk down the aisle alone behind your attendants. I hope you don't choose this last idea, however, because when your knees and hands are shaking, sturdy male biceps come in real handy!

What percentage of marriages today are second marriages?
Approximately 30 percent.

What are some things we should take into consideration when setting our wedding date?
Here are just a few:

- Saturday is the most popular day of the week to be married because it is so convenient for the guests.
- If you're planning a civil ceremony in a judge's office, the wedding date will have to be a weekday because city offices aren't open on weekends.
- You will want to select a date that conveniently precedes the vacation days you have coming at work and coincides with your honeymoon plans.
- You may want to set the date in consideration of the bride's menstrual cycle.
- Select a date that does not conflict with other special family occasions, such as a birthday, anniversary or bar mitzvah.
- Select a date that is acceptable in your religious faith. For example, Christians usually don't marry on a Sunday and Jews never marry on the Sabbath (Friday sundown to Saturday sundown).
- Select a time of day most suitable to your budget. Morning and afternoon weddings are usually less formal and require less elaborate food and drink. Evening weddings with formal sit-down dinners are the most expensive.

My sister and I have always been very close. I know she wants to be my maid of honor, but I really prefer to ask my best friend instead and have my sister as a bridesmaid. I don't want to hurt my sister's feelings. Any suggestions?
Yes. Did you know that you can have two maids of honor or two matrons of honor or one of each? They should stand

side-by-side when attending you during the wedding. One may be responsible to straighten your veil and train and hold your finance's ring; the other may hold your bouquet during the ceremony. So that your guests understand that you have two maids of honor, be sure their names are listed as such in your ceremony program. In the case of one maid of honor and one matron of honor, which is perfectly acceptable as well, the maid of honor always takes precedence, being the last attendant to walk down the aisle.

Can my mother be my matron of honor?
Of course. A bride has the right to choose anyone she wants as her honor attendant, including her mother, an aunt or even her grandmother, if she wishes.

My fiance and I are tied up with our work schedules, so we plan to be married over a three-day weekend. What can we do to simplify things in the days leading up to the wedding?
Many working couples are forced to work a wedding weekend into their busy schedules, and although this is not ideal, it is possible. Here are some things you can do to ease the last-minute anxieties:

- Limit the number of prewedding activities—there will be time to party after the wedding.
- Start planning your wedding as soon as possible, doing everything you can in advance. For example, assemble as many of the decorations as you can, bake and freeze finger foods for the reception and make up the men's boutonnieres and the women's bouquets in silk flowers.
- Delegate, delegate, delegate. If anyone asks, "Is there anything I can do to help?", be ready with a list of duties.
- Limit the number of bridal attendants—the fewer, the less chance of last minute problems with fittings, transportation, etc.

My cousin hired a professional wedding coordinator to help plan her wedding. How much does one of these consultants cost, and isn't it possible to save the money by doing everything ourselves?

There are several types of wedding coordinators, from the consultant provided by a church or synagogue for a minimal fee to the department store employee working on commission to the full-service professional who charges hourly rates or a 10 to 15 percent fee which is included in the total cost of the wedding.

There are several types of these full-service professionals, as well: the *bridal consultant* who helps plan and coordinate the wedding, sometimes in conjunction with a vendor, such as a florist or caterer; a *wedding coordinator* who not only helps plan and coordinate the wedding, but actually supervises the wedding activities, as well; and a *wedding day coordinator* who works with you to see that the plans you have already made on your own are carried out during the rehearsal and the day of the wedding itself. To confuse things even further, any of these professionals may also be called a *wedding director*, *wedding consultant* or *wedding professional*.

If you or your mother are an organized person, however, you are perfectly capable of planning the wedding yourself. All you need is a fat three-ring notebook with about a ream of lined paper, divided into sections—one section for every category: the budget, the calendar, the ceremony, the reception, the wedding attire, the flowers, the photography and videography, the food, the music, the decorations and the incidental expenses. Use the notebook to keep track of every aspect of the wedding, from prices to people to procedures to preferences. Be sure to jot down every telephone call, every bid, every promise made, every selection, etc. Staying organized is the key to coordinating a wedding. Just don't lose the notebook!

If we were to hire a professional to help us, how do we find a reputable one?

First of all, you need to realize that there are dozens of people out there claiming to be wedding consultants, from DJs who play at wedding receptions to the sales clerks who work on commission at the bridal salons of large department stores. What you want is a trained full-time professional. Look in your yellow pages for wedding consultants who are members of the Association of Bridal Consultants; if you can't find one in your yellow pages, call their national association office at 203-355-0464 for the names of members in your area.

What exactly will one of these professionals do for us?

Here are some of the services they provide:

- Helping you select ceremony and reception sites, plus all the vendors (flowers, food, music, photography, etc.) suitable to your theme, personalities and budget.
- Ensuring communication between these vendors (so that the florist knows what your bridal gown looks like as he designs your bouquet, etc.).
- Serving you as financial advisor, counselor, etiquette expert, referee and friend.
- Seeing that your dreams come true and your rehearsal and wedding day run smoothly.

You can hire a bridal consultant the day you become engaged to coordinate everything from day one, or you can hire her near the end of the planning process—a couple months before the wedding day—just to pull everything together and oversee the rehearsal and wedding day activities. One of these professionals is a *must* if you're trying to plan a long-distance wedding or, as with so many career women these days, you're already on overload at work and don't have the time to plan a large wedding.

Are bridal consultants always women?

According to the Association of Bridal Consultants, only 2 percent are men.

A big wedding is sounding more expensive all the time, not to say anything of the time and effort to plan it. Doesn't anyone elope anymore?

Funny you should ask because, as a matter of fact, many couples are deciding to do just that, with an informal reception hosted by the bride's parents after they get back from their honeymoon. It has even become a fad to be married in a simple civil ceremony at the honeymoon destination, saving the cost of a big wedding. Another clever, economical way to be married is to plan it as a surprise. One couple pulled this off beautifully by having the bride's parents invite an unusually large crowd of friends and relatives for Thanksgiving dinner, including the groom's parents, brothers and their wives. Then, two hours before dinner, their minister arrived to perform the surprise wedding ceremony. After the sumptuous meal, which also served as their wedding feast, the couple left on their four-day Thanksgiving holiday honeymoon. With this ingenious plan, they were married for the cost of their minister's fee yet surrounded by the loving members of their immediate family.

The same type of surprise wedding worked for another couple, as well—this time at what was supposed to be a simple Christmas party. They invited only their closest and dearest friends to this party and then right in the middle of it, the stereo switched from playing Christmas music to "The Wedding March." No one paid much attention at first until, finally, as the music became louder and louder everyone finally stopped talking, a minister and the couple stepped forward and the short ceremony began. Evidently, the guests were absolutely speechless and were caught completely off guard. Needless to say, the party ended with many tears of congratulations.

Do any of these weddings give you ideas?

How young is too young when it comes to including a child as part of the wedding party?

Many bridal consultants feel that any younger than 4 is probably too young; however, I have seen younger children than that participate, but after the child has (hopefully) made it down the aisle, he or she sits with an adult in one of the front rows, thus avoiding anything too cute that may distract from the bride and groom during the ceremony.

What is a "destination wedding"?

This is a wedding that takes place at your honeymoon destination; it is also known as a *travel wedding* or a *honeymoon wedding*. The reason some couples prefer a destination wedding is that it is often less expensive and complex than a full-blown ceremony and reception back home. The guests, usually only your close friends, members of the wedding party and members of your "inner family," customarily pay their own way to the site, although the families of the bride and groom may certainly pick up the tab, if they wish. If a destination wedding sounds like a good idea to you, here are some suggestions to make the planning run smoothly:

- Hire a full-service bridal consultant in your destination city or at your honeymoon hotel who will make *all* the arrangements.
- Find a full-service travel agent who will not only make all the travel arrangements for you and your guests, but will also keep your guests informed (provide updated itineraries, etc.)
- If you plan to bring the wedding gown with you on the plane, bring it in a hanging bag (don't check through baggage). Make arrangements ahead of time to have any wrinkles steamed out once you're at your destination.
- Create a newsletter for all your guests informing them of all the travel and wedding plans, including schedules, costs, etc. You may want to include a brochure of the hotel and tourist information for the destination—provided by your travel agent.

What are some of the most common destinations for one of these "honeymoon weddings"?

You can select any destination you would like, as long as it has the room to accommodate your wedding and reception. However, these are some popular choices:

- Disneyland in California or Disney World in Florida, both of which provide a Cinderella Coach, complete with a footman and six white horses!
- A cruise ship provides a romantic "destination wedding" site, although couples are usually married at dockside by an authorized officiant since, contrary to popular belief, most ships' captains are *not* legally authorized to perform wedding services.
- Las Vegas is actually a relatively inexpensive choice, and they are *totally* prepared to marry you, believe me.
- The most popular choice of all is Hawaii with its dependable climate year-round and abundance of romantic settings.

What if we were to be married in a foreign country? Would our marriage be legal in the United States?

Yes, as long as the marriage conforms to the rules of that country. Here are some questions you should ask in order to assure its legality:

- What documentation is required?
- What medical tests are required?
- What is the processing time to obtain a marriage license?
- Is there a waiting period after the license has been issued?
- Are there religious rules or restrictions?

We like the idea of a destination wedding because we will be saving all the hoopla and expense of a full-blown wedding at home, but we don't think many of our family members or friends can afford to fly to Hawaii for a wedding, and we can't afford to pay their way or we'll be back where we started from financially. Any solutions?

Yes. Do what so many couples do: get married at their destination with the witnesses provided for them at their ceremony site. Then, they let their parents host a reception for them when they get back from their honeymoon.

If we do this, can I wear my wedding gown to the reception?

Absolutely!

What is a "progressive wedding"?

It is a wedding with a series of receptions that take place in different places and/or cities. For example, you may be married in your home town, then travel to your reception site nearby, then the next day to your parents' home town for another reception, then to your groom's parents' home town for a third reception, then, finally, to the homes of various friends and relatives for what might be called *afterglows* (see Chapter 20). A progressive wedding takes a great deal of planning, as you can imagine, and it can become quite tiring for everyone involved. Many couples choose this type of celebration, however, in an effort to appease their scattered friends and relatives. It is *exactly* the opposite of a simple little wedding!

What is an "all-night wedding"?

It is an all-night extravaganza that begins with the ceremony around 10 p.m. and carries through with dancing and partying until the first rays of sunlight. The cake isn't cut until about 4 a.m., followed by an early wedding breakfast. Often an all-night wedding is planned for New Year's

Eve. It works best to hold one of these marathons at a hotel with a couple of dozen rooms reserved for those guests who need to "nap" off and on in order to keep up their strength.

What is a "costume wedding"?

A costume wedding is one whose theme lends itself to wearing costumes, such as a Henry VIII English Tudor wedding, a Renaissance, Medieval or Folk wedding, a Halloween or Masked Ball wedding, a Western, Polynesian, Guys 'n' Dolls, Romeo and Juliet, Elizabethan, Victorian, Edwardian, Greco-Roman or Southern Antebellum wedding, or any ethnic wedding. These weddings are complicated and time-consuming to plan; in fact, they practically become theatrical productions. Costumes for these weddings may be sewn from patterns, rented from a costume shop, borrowed from a theatrical production company or, in the case of Elizabethan, Victorian and Edwardian themes, the costumes may be purchased through catalogs available at many bridal salons.

Are there advantages to having the ceremony and reception at the same site?

I've spoken with many wedding coordinators who swear there are countless advantages to having them at the same location: easier on everyone concerned; less expensive; eliminates providing a limo or other transportation for the wedding party from one site to another; and requires less time overall so you won't tend to "lose" guests between the ceremony and reception.

Can I somehow include my dog as part of the ceremony?

Dogs have served as *ring bearers, flower girls* and, in one case I know of, as the groom's *best man.* In that particular case the dog sat still beside the groom, perfectly behaved throughout the entire service. What I wonder, however, is what happens if the dog *isn't* well-behaved?

Chapter 4

The Bridal Registry

What is a bridal registry?

Remember when you were a kid and you made a list for Santa? Well, this is the same idea, only you're much more likely to receive the gifts on *this* list. A bridal gift registry is a free service offered by department stores, jewelry stores and gift shops; it is delightfully advantageous for the bride and groom, as well as the shoppers themselves. The stores provide forms for you to fill out as you select everything from china pattern, to crystal, to linens, to housewares, to silver, to luggage. Most department stores enter this information into a user-friendly computer that can be accessed by shoppers who are looking for gift ideas.

Don't be afraid to select a few outrageously expensive gifts, such as an oriental rug or a piece of artwork, because it's quite common for several people to go together on one really nice gift. As each gift is purchased, it is removed from the master list so that, ideally, you will receive just the right number of each thing. By the way, allow plenty of time to register for your gifts so you won't feel rushed, and be sure to enjoy this special time in your lives—it's the only time "wishes" truly become "horses."

What are the basic gifts we should register for at a department store? And how many of each item?

Here is a list of the basics, but you should know that you can register for *anything* the store carries, whether it seems to be a traditional wedding gift or not.

Flatware:

You may register for sets of sterling silver, silver plate or stainless steel or for all three. Each place setting should consist of:

- Dinner knife.
- Dinner fork.
- Lunch fork (also called a salad or dessert fork).
- Dessert spoon.
- Butter knife.
- Table knife.
- Teaspoon.

In addition, you may also want to register for serving spoons, butter server, ice tea spoons, soup spoons, gravy ladle, pickle forks and cake server.

China or everyday dishes:
- 8 dinner plates.
- 8 dessert plates.
- 8 cereal bowls.
- 8 butter plates.
- 1 serving platter.
- 2 serving bowls.
- Sugar bowl and cream pitcher.

Glass or crystal:
- 8 water goblets.
- 8 all-purpose wine glasses.
- 8 cocktail glasses.
- 8 tumblers.

Bed linen:

- 4 sets of sheets and pillowcases for each bed.
- Mattress pads for each bed.
- One summer and one winter blanket per bed.

Bath linen:

- 6 towels, hand towels and washcloths for each bathroom.
- 2 bath mats for each bathroom.
- Shower curtain, as needed.
- 2 sets of guest towels.

Table linen:

- 8 linen place mats with matching napkins.
- 1 linen or damask tablecloth with matching napkins.
- 3 everyday tablecloths with matching napkins.
- 3 sets of everyday place mats with matching napkins.

Kitchen linen:

- Decorative tea towels and potholders.
- Kitchen equipment: Register for anything and everything you see in the store, including pots and pans, mixing bowls, baking pans and dishes, measuring cups, rolling pin, colander, sifter, grater, spatulas, knives, ice-cream scoops, can opener, corkscrew, blender, toaster, breadboard, coffee makers, canister set, etc.

A word of advice when it comes to registries: Select gifts in a variety of price ranges so that your guests won't feel intimidated by a list that only contains expensive items.

What are some of the most popular gifts couples register for?

Well, in addition to the basics, here are the five most popular selections:

- A down comforter.
- VCR.
- Microwave oven.
- Vacuum cleaner.
- Slow cooker.

What if we receive incomplete sets of the things we have registered for?

You can fill in the sets by purchasing the missing pieces with money you have received as wedding gifts, or you may return the incomplete sets and trade them for one or two single gifts or one complete set of something you really need.

My fiance doesn't seem interested in picking out our china pattern, and he doesn't feel comfortable with the whole idea of a gift registry. Any suggestions?

This is quite common so don't let it become a problem between the two of you. Take your sister or your best friend with you to help make your selections, then tell your fiance all about it later. If he *should* acquire an interest in what you've selected and wants to see for himself, you can casually drop by the store some day to show him your choices. You see, it isn't that he won't appreciate the gifts and enjoy using the new blender, coffee grinder or ecru peach towels, it's just that some men get about as excited over a gift registry as you would over buying a new set of tires.

Aren't there some places where my fiance can register for gifts?

Boy, are there ever! In fact, it has become quite the thing for the groom to register at camping and mountaineering stores, hardware stores, home improvement stores, garden stores, cycling stores and travel agencies. By registering at a travel agency he may be able to afford a much nicer honeymoon for the two of you.

What about registering for a down payment on a house?

Many couples are registering at mortgage companies for their down payments. A mortgage officer on the East Coast said that whenever this type of gift registry is established at his company the couple receives anywhere from $1,000 to $25,000.

What happens if a gift arrives broken or damaged?

If you know where it was purchased, take it back and ask for a replacement. The important thing is that the donor never be told about the problem, but write a lovely thank-you note anyway and never breathe a word about it. Only in the case where a broken or damaged gift arrived fully insured should you contact the giver.

When should we register?

As soon as you've set your wedding date. That way the registries can be used for prewedding showers and engagement parties as well.

What if we receive duplicate gifts?

Exchange one of them for something else, but it is not necessary to tell the donors you did so. Simply write a thank-you note for each of the gifts.

Chapter 5

Who Pays for What?

What does a wedding cost these days, anyway? I've heard some astronomical figures.

It depends on where you live; the metropolitan areas of California and the Northeast are the most expensive, while the central mountain states (Montana, Nebraska, Utah, South Dakota, North Dakota and Wyoming) are the least. According to a recent survey, however, the average cost of a wedding in the United States is approximately $18,000.

How do these costs break down, percentage-wise?

The reception food and drink are the highest expenses of any wedding, running from 30 to 50 percent of the total, depending on the size of the wedding. However, an average wedding costing $18,000 would break down like this:

Reception food and drink	50% of total cost	$9,000
Bride's attire	10%	$1,800
Photography	10%	$1,800
Music	10%	$1,800
Flowers	10%	$1,800
Miscellaneous (decorations, transportation, parking attendants, thank-you notes, garter, ring pillow, guest book, clergyman's fee, etc.)	6%	$1,080
Invitations and postage	4%	$720

Note: Every wedding is different; there are no set rules about expenditures. Many couples would prefer to spend less on the reception, for example, and use the savings for their honeymoon. Or the bride may fall in love with a $3,000 gown and squeeze that money out of the floral and music funds. It all depends on each couple's priorities.

Is there a way to figure the average cost per guest?

As a very general rule of thumb, figure on $100 per guest. For example, a $10,000 wedding would have 100 guests, and a $30,000 wedding, 300 guests.

What are the expenses of the bride's family?

Before we get started on this lengthy list, let me say that who pays for what is no longer a hard, fast rule, especially with the enormous expenses involved with weddings to-day. With the exception that the groom usually pays for the bride's rings, and the bride for the groom's, all of the rest of the expenses may be shared. I've seen situations where the bride's family was not in a financial position to pay for a large, expensive wedding, but the groom's family was and they sincerely wanted to help out with the costs. With the right attitude on the part of everyone involved, this shouldn't be a problem. I have seen other situations where a grandmother or aunt offered to pay for everything as a sort of preinheritance gift. However, here is the *traditional* list of expenses expected to be paid by the bride's family:

- The engagement party.
- The wedding gown and trousseau.
- The cost of a wedding consultant, if one is hired.
- Wedding invitations/announcements/ceremony programs, etc.
- Rental of the ceremony and reception sites.
- Decoration of both sites.

- Fees for the musicians.
- Transportation of the bridesmaids to the ceremony and reception.
- The entire cost of the reception, including the cake, food, beverages, caterer's fees, tips, etc.
- All photography, including the bride's engagement photograph.
- Lodging for the out-of-town bridesmaids.
- All flowers (except for those worn by the bride, groom, groomsmen, parents and grandparents).

What are the traditional expenses of the groom and his family?

- The bride's rings.
- The marriage license.
- The clergyman's fee.
- Rehearsal dinner/party.
- His wedding attire.
- Gifts for the best man, groomsmen and ushers.
- Boutonnieres for the groom, the best man, his attendants, both fathers and grandfathers.
- The bride's bouquet and going-away corsage.
- Corsages for both mothers and all grandmothers.

We only have $4,000 to spend on our wedding; how much of this $4,000 should go toward each expense?

Rather than give you my personal suggestions, perhaps it would be more helpful (and encouraging) to you if I give you the *actual* cost breakdown of a wedding that took place recently in Butte, Montana, with 250 guests. First, I'll list their actual expenses, and then I'll tell you how they did it.

The Best Wedding Ever

Bride's gown	$400
Bride's makeup	0
Rented hoop petticoat	8
Veil	15
Shoes and hosiery	30
Rented bridesmaids' gowns	50
Gifts for the attendants	120
Reception hall rental	250
Photographer	265
Wedding cake	150
Videotaping	0
Caterer	675
DJ for the reception	0
Organist	15
Soloist	15
Trumpeters (2)	120
Flowers	200
Decorations, balloons, etc.	100
Men's attire	150
Misc.	600
Total:	**$3,388**

Now, let me tell you how they pulled this off:

Bride's gown	Sewn by a seamstress in Seattle.
Bride's makeup	Done at no charge by a friend of the bride.
Veil	The bride made it herself.
Shoes and hosiery	Purchased at a discount store.
Bridesmaids' gowns	Bride split cost of renting them.
Attendants' gifts	Shopped wisely and found them for $20 each.
Minister's fee	No charge (father of the bride!).
Photography	Ordered a minimal package from a retired photographer and supplemented it with photographs taken by the bride's sister-in-law.

Wedding cake	Ordered from a woman who makes cakes in her own home.
Videotaping	No charge (brother of the bride!).
Caterer	A friend of the bride's mother who runs a catering service out of her home, but only charged them her cost (as a wedding gift).
Musicians	Friends of the bride's mother who offered to perform for free, but bride bought them thank-you gifts.
Flowers	The bride made up all the flower arrangements, boutonnieres, corsages and bouquets months ahead of time in silks that she purchased at a discount market.
Decorations	Used donated and borrowed decorations and supplemented with lots of balloons.

Although the wedding took place in Montana, most of the supplies were purchased in Seattle.

Every successful *budget wedding* has its own story, and I have received literally hundreds of them as brides and grooms have written to me after reading my books or attending my seminars. Obviously, in order to have a quality wedding on a small budget, you will need to do a lot of the work yourself, and you will also need the good fortune of having friends and family members willing to donate their time and talents. You might want to pick up a copy of my book *How to Have a Big Wedding on a Small Budget,* which will be a big help in keeping your costs down. The encouraging thing is that you *can* have a lovely wedding for $4,000, although your spending priorities may be quite different from the budget just described.

Chapter 6

Inviting the Guests

How do we go about compiling our guest list? Is there some rule of thumb?

Yes, there are several. Here they are:

The size of the guest list is determined by whoever is paying for the wedding; the number of invitations is usually split evenly between the bride's and groom's parents; an invitation to any married guest *always* includes the spouse; everyone who participates in the wedding should be invited to the reception, along with the spouse; the addressing of the invitations is the responsibility of the bride's family.

What is the difference between "engraving," "thermography" and "lithography"?

Engraving is the more traditional type of printing technique that results in raised print that is pressed through and can be felt on the back of the paper; thermography also results in raised print, but the print is shinier, less expensive and is not "pressed through" the paper. Lithography, which imprints the lettering with ink and does not result in raised or pressed-through letters, is the least costly technique of all and is perfectly acceptable to be used for wedding invitations.

What is the traditional wording for a formal wedding invitation?

Here is an example of a formal invitation:

> *Mr. and Mrs. James Hubert Smith*
> *request the honour of your presence*
> *at the marriage of their daughter*
> *Emily Suzanne*
> *to*
> *Mr. Winston Carter Jones*
> *Saturday, the fourth of May*
> *at two o'clock*
> *Church of the Wildwood*
> *San Andreas, Oregon*

My father passed away two years ago, so my mother will be paying for the wedding. How should we word the invitations?

Word it just the same as the one shown above, except in place of "Mr. and Mrs. James Hubert Smith," say, "Mrs. James Hubert Smith." (A formal invitation must use her husband's name, but an informal invitation may say "Mrs. Susie Smith" instead.)

I have a different problem. My mother was widowed several years ago, but has remarried, and both of them are paying for the wedding. How do we word the invitation so that it is understood that I am her daughter?

There is a simple change in the wording whereby you are shown to be *her* daughter; here is an example:

> *Mr. and Mrs. Donald Eugene Swenson*
> *request the honour of your presence*
> *at the marriage of her daughter*
> *Melinda Sue Anderson*

etc.

The inclusion of your last name will also prevent any misunderstanding. By the way, the same rule applies for a father who has been widowed and then remarried: the wording states "at the marriage of *his* daughter."

Here's another one of those "divorced and remarried" questions. My parents divorced years ago and have both remarried. The problem is that both of my parents want to give me this wedding. How should their names be worded on the invitation?

Using the same format shown above for a formal invitation, simply include the names of both couples:

> *Mr. and Mrs. Henry Andrew Knapp*
> *and*
> *Mr. and Mrs. Ronald John Melville*
>
> etc.

My parents are deceased and my fiance's parents are giving us our wedding. What do we do about the wording?

Here is an example of the proper wording. Notice that your name is preceded by "Miss" and the "Mr." is dropped from your fiance's name.

> *Mr. and Mrs. Steven Francis Brownell*
> *request the honor of your presence*
> *at the marriage of*
> *Miss Diana Henderson*
> *to their son*
> *Charles Gordon Brownell*
>
> etc.

My sister and I are being married in a double ceremony. How should the invitations be worded?

Here is the proper wording for an invitation to a double wedding:

> *Mr. and Mrs. Richard Allan Burkett*
> *request the honour of your presence*
> *at the marriage of their daughters*
> *Sheryl Anne*
> *to*
> *Mr. James Carter Patterson*
> *and*
> *Denise Lynne*
> *to*
> *Mr. Paul Ronald Vinson*

We are sending out our own invitations. How should they read?

If the parents aren't involved, their names should be omitted from the invitations altogether. Here is the proper wording:

> *The honour of your presence*
> *is requested at the marriage of*
> *Miss Barbara Jane Banks*
> *to*
> *Mr. Jason Harold Johnson*

Is the wording any different for a civil ceremony?

The only difference is that you would use the less formal wording of "the pleasure of your company" in place of "the honour of your company."

What is the proper way to address the two envelopes?

Unfortunately, you are required to write everyone's name twice, once on the outer sealed envelope, along with the full address, and once on the inner unsealed envelope. Here is an example of the full name and address for the outer envelope:

Mr. and Mrs. George Edward Johnson
2527 Elmwood Avenue
Indianapolis, Indiana 46202

And then, on the inner envelope, write simply:

Mr. and Mrs. Johnson

If you don't know the guest's full middle name, omit it rather than use an initial.

We have several friends who are separated, but not divorced as yet. How do we address their wedding invitations?

Whether they are officially divorced yet or not, it is best to be safe and send separate invitations.

Should we order printed engagement announcements?

It's considered poor taste to send engraved or printed engagement announcements; instead, write personal notes to your relatives and close friends, or give them a call. Once they have heard the good news directly from you it is all right to have the engagement announced in your local newspaper.

How much time should be allowed to have our invitations printed?

If your invitations are being engraved or thermographed, allow at least three months. Actually, it doesn't hurt to order them as soon as you have confirmed your ceremony and reception sites and times. This is a wonderful insurance against last-minute wedding anxiety in case the printer doesn't get them to you as promised, or in case they arrive with a heartbreaking typo that wasn't caught before they went to print.

When should we mail our invitations?

It depends on whether the wedding is formal or informal. A formal wedding requires that the invitations be mailed at least a month in advance, preferably six weeks. Two to three weeks is fine for an informal wedding.

Since the reception is the biggest expense of a wedding, we have decided to limit the number of wedding guests who will be invited to the reception. How do we do this in a tactful way?

The best way is to include a separate invitation to the reception inside your wedding invitation only for those designated guests. It would be a nice touch, by the way, to form a receiving line at the back of the ceremony site after the wedding so that all the guests may greet you and wish you well, since they won't all be able to do so at the reception.

We are planning a small wedding in the garden of my family's home which will be limited to the wedding party and our closest relatives, but we would like to have a large reception for all our friends and extended family. How do we word the invitations?

This is very simply handled by sending invitations only to the reception; no explanation is needed as to where or when the wedding itself took place.

What does the term "within the ribbon" mean?

It means that the guests who receive an enclosure card with these words imprinted on it within the wedding invitation should sit in one of the pews designated for them, usually decorated in a special way with ribbons or flowers. The ushers should be alerted that anyone handing them a card with the words *within the ribbon* should be escorted to these designated pews.

What are "enclosure cards"?

Enclosure cards are small cards enclosed inside a wedding invitation; there are various reasons for these cards. A *pew card* is one that reserves a seat in a specific row, such as *within the ribbon*; an *at-home card* is a small card, usually three by four inches, that gives the bride's new address after she is married; a *response card*, the most common enclosure, is what is known as an *R.S.V.P. card* that the guests are requested to fill out and return indicating whether or not they will be able to attend the reception; a *reception card* is inserted only into the invitations of those guests who are invited to the reception following the ceremony; a *map card* is a small card that gives directions to the ceremony and/or reception sites; a *rain card* is a small card that gives the alternate locations for the wedding and/or reception in case of rain. For example, a rain card may read: *"In case of rain the wedding and reception will be held in the Civic Center Senior Hall at 101 North Blake Street."*

By the way, if you want to adhere strictly to the rules of etiquette, omit the response cards because they are considered to be in very poor taste. Nevertheless, they are quite common these days because of people's busy schedules and their lack of response to the traditional R.S.V.P., which requests telephoning a reply.

What does "R.S.V.P." actually mean, anyway?

It is French for *repondez s'il vous plait*, which means "please respond."

How can we keep track of these responses?

I suggest you make up a list with columns (preferably in your computer) with these headings:

- Date invitation sent.
- Name and address of guest.
- Response (Yes, No, How many?).
- Shower gift received?
- Thank-you sent?
- Wedding gift received?
- Thank-you sent?

By adding gift information to this master list you will not only have everything together, but you'll have each guest's address handy for writing the thank-you's.

Is it acceptable to list the names of the stores where we have registered on the bottom of the invitation, or as an insert?

Sorry, but it is never acceptable under any circumstances. You'll have to depend on word of mouth to let your guests know where you are registered. Usually, guests will call and ask; that's what I always do. Or you can include a list of stores in the bridal shower invitation.

We are going to have a very small wedding. Would it be proper to call the guests to extend the invitations? Or possibly send handwritten notes?

Either would be fine. Here is sample wording for a simple handwritten invitation:

Dear Ben and Ginny,

Jack and I are going to be married at Christ Community Church on July 10 at 3 o'clock. We hope you will be able to come and then join us afterward for a light supper reception on the patio of my parents' home at 3210 Loyola Avenue.

With much love,

Melinda

My fiance's parents feel obligated to invite many of their business acquaintances who have invited them to their children's weddings, but I only want guests I know and love at my wedding. Is this common for invitations to be sent to so many people the bride doesn't even know?

Unfortunately, it is quite common and there probably isn't anything you can do about it. I have strong personal feelings against this type of thing where wedding invitations are sent to fulfill business obligations. A wedding ceremony is a sacred, personal occasion, and I think the bride and groom have the right to be surrounded only by loving friends and relatives who are there to support them and celebrate with them.

Is it proper to state on the invitation what the guests can expect in the way of food?

Yes. It is not only proper but a very good idea to let your guests know what to expect, especially if the reception falls close to a normal meal time. You can inform them tactfully by merely adding, in small italicized letters at the bottom of the invitation, the words: *Dinner reception to follow* or *Hors d'oeuvres reception to follow*. That way, your guests know how much to eat before the wedding, saving room for the feast or filling up before the famine.

We have limited space for our reception. Would it be all right if we invite only a certain number of guests to the reception, but let the others know that if there are any cancellations, we will contact them?

Absolutely not! This would be *really* tacky! Either invite a guest to the reception or not; the alternative would be taken as a great insult by those who are not invited at first.

What is an "open church" invitation?

It is an invitation to everyone who attends the bride's or groom's church. Usually, the invitation is announced from the pulpit, printed in the church bulletin and also in the weekly or monthly church newsletter that goes to each member's home. This is what we did with our daughter's wedding and it resulted in about 100 more guests than we had planned! Scary!

Chapter 7

The Bride

What is the average price paid for a wedding gown today?

It varies around the country, with higher prices in the Northeast, southern California and the larger cities, but the overall average is approximately $800 for the gown, plus $150 for the headpiece and veil and another $200 to $600 for the undergarments and accessories, for a grand total of about $1,400.

My Mom and I went shopping for my wedding gown for the first time last Saturday and by the end of the day I was thoroughly confused. The sales people used terms like "formal daytime" and "semiformal evening." All I know is that I want a floor-length gown. Are there strict rules on the length of a bridal gown?

You are the bride and you may select any dress you wish; however, if you want to at least consider the rules of wedding etiquette, keep these three things in mind: A floor-length gown is suitable for any wedding, day or night, as long as the wedding is formal or semiformal; for a very formal wedding, the gown should have a train and the bride usually wears a veil; for an informal wedding, whether day or night, you may wear a street-length dinner dress, a short cocktail dress, a suit or a very simple ankle-length wedding gown without a face veil.

I'm not too crazy about wearing a veil at all. What are some other choices?

You may wear a single flower or a wreath of flowers in your hair, or you may wear a simple bow on the back of your head or even a bridal hat. You may also decide to wear nothing on your head at all, which is fine unless there is a religious reason why your head should be covered. For example, all brides being married in Orthodox Jewish ceremonies must be veiled.

I'm going to be wearing a long cathedral-length veil. How do I handle it during the reception?

The best solution is to have your veil made so that it is detachable from your headpiece. Have your maid of honor on hand to rescue your veil and store it in a safe place until after your honeymoon.

This is my second marriage. Will it be in bad taste for me to wear white?

Of course not! You may wear a traditional white wedding gown or a gown of any color you would like. There are a couple of rules you may wish to follow, however, when it comes to your attire: A second-time bride usually doesn't wear a veil nor does her dress have a train.

I found a gown I just love, but it is a pale peach color; my sister says that color is only for second brides. Is that true?

No, not at all. The modern brides of the 90s often choose pale pinks and peaches, as well as varied shades of ivory, cream and off-white. It depends a great deal on your coloring. Many women don't look their best in a stark white-white and are wise to choose a more becoming color.

I'm having trouble deciding on how to style my hair for the wedding. I want it to be something special. Are there any guidelines?

The first thing you need to do is purchase your headpiece and veil because that will determine how you should wear your hair. Take it with you to your hair salon and ask for the advice of your stylist. Also, check out the models in bridal magazines; look for those wearing veils like yours.

Not only am I short, but I'm also short-waisted. What style gown would be best for me?

I've received so many questions asking what style dress is best for each type of figure, let me answer all of them here, including yours:

- **Short and short-waisted.** Look for a petite-sized princess-style gown with simple sleeves and neckline.
- **Tall.** Look for a gown with flared or tiered skirts and a defined neckline.
- **Plus-sized.** Look for a princess-style gown with simple lines and embroidery, lace or pearl detail near the neckline.
- **Big bosomed.** Look for a gown with a high neckline and a dropped waistline.
- **Thin.** Look for a full gown with ruffles, shoulder pads and lots of detail work.

I'm on a diet and plan to lose another 20 pounds before the wedding, but I need to order my gown now. Should I buy one or two sizes smaller than my present size?

I know you plan to lose this weight, and I'm sure you will. However, just to be safe, order your gown to fit you today. Then, if you do lose this weight, have the gown taken in. It's impossible to alter a size 10 into a size 14.

When should I order my gown to allow plenty of time for alterations?

Order your dress as soon as possible, preferably six to nine months before the wedding. It should arrive three to four months after you place the order, allowing plenty of time for three fittings: the first fitting as soon as it arrives; the second one month before the wedding; and the third two weeks before the wedding. If you can't order your gown at least six months before the wedding, find one off the rack, at a discount warehouse or through a JCPenney's catalog, even if it is a size or two larger than you wanted. You can always have the gown altered and that way you'll at least be assured of having a gown in time for your wedding with no ugly surprises at the last minute when your order doesn't arrive in time. Another option if there is a time crunch, of course, is to have your gown fashioned for you by a professional seamstress.

I would really like to find a gown that fits me, that I like, off the rack, but all the salons I've visited have only a limited number in stock; they always suggest I place an order for a certain gown in my size. Is there any such place as one store that has a huge selection of gowns on hand, ready to be purchased on the spot?

There is a store called Kleinfeld's on 82nd Street in Brooklyn, New York, which is said to be the largest bridal shop in the world. It has 30,000 square feet stocked with 3,000 gowns. Brides go there from all over the world to select their gowns, with the help of the shop's bridal consultants. I know of a bride from my own area here in California who flew out there with a budget of less than $1,000 to spend on a gown; she found one on their bargain rack for less than $900—it was a Bianchi silk shantung gown that fit her perfectly! Of course, not many brides can afford to fly all over the country shopping for their weddings, although it sounds like a lot of fun!

You said that bride found a gown for less than $1,000, but what does the average bride spend for a gown at Kleinfeld's?

Between $1,500 and $2,000.

Why does the bride carry a bridal handkerchief?

It is considered a "lucky" thing to do. The tradition dates back to the days when farmers believed a bride's wedding day tears were lucky and would bring rain for their crops. Also, an old wives' tale said that if a bride cried at her wedding, she would never shed another tear.

What should I pack up to take with me when I go to the church to dress for the ceremony?

In addition to your gown, headpiece, shoes, purse, slip, jewelry, bra, garters and pantyhose, you'll need an emergency kit with the following:

- An extra pair of pantyhose.
- Hand mirror.
- Makeup.
- Hair fixings, including hairspray, hairpins, combs, lifters, etc.
- Nail file and nail polish.
- Safety pins (all sizes).
- Complete sewing kit.
- Masking tape (white).
- Box of tissues.
- Hand towel and wash cloth.
- Static cling spray (a must-bring-along).
- Bottled water or small cans of juice.
- Breath mints and mouthwash.
- Sanitary napkins.
- Scissors.
- Super-adhesive glue.

- Stapler.
- Deodorant.
- Hand lotion.
- Bottle of aspirin, acetaminophen or ibuprofen.
- First aid supplies, including small adhesive bandages.
- Baby powder.
- Cleaning fluids (one for water-soluble and one for greasy stains).
- Spare contact lens and lens fluid.
- Towelettes.
- Transparent tape.

Words of caution: After you've been working with your makeup and hairspray, etc. don't even think about touching your gown until you've washed your hands. Also, when slipping your gown over your head be careful that it doesn't rub against your makeup.

I would like to try to make my own veil. Where do I start?

More brides should give this idea a try. The cost of the materials that go into making a bridal headpiece are so small in comparison to paying full retail price in a salon that it is certainly worth the effort. The first time I tried to make a veil I spent about $16 on the materials for a copy of one I had seen in a bridal salon for $175. I made it without a pattern, purchasing the silk flowers, stems already wrapped with satin, from a floral supply store, and the tulle netting from a fabric store. It took me less than an hour to make it and it turned out so well I had brides in my seminars begging to purchase it. Give it a try and even if it doesn't work out, you will be out very little money for the effort. You can purchase a veil pattern, by the way, at any fabric store, or you may use my pattern and instructions from my book entitled *Beautiful Wedding Decorations and Gifts on a Small Budget*.

I'd like to make my own wedding dress, but I'm not quite confident enough to give it a try. Is there a way I can get some help?

You might try a compromise: Pay an experienced seamstress to sew up the shell and then do all the detailed finish work yourself. After all, it's the finish work that runs up the bill, so you can save a great deal of money by sewing on the pearls, sequins and lace. Another suggestion, by the way, is to start with a very simple, very plain ready-made wedding gown or bridesmaid's gown and then embellish it in the same way.

How many brides actually wear their mothers' wedding gowns?

Statistics say that fewer than 4 percent of today's brides wear their mothers' gowns.

What is the most popular style of veil?

The most popular style is the *fingertip veil* which hangs just to the tips of the bride's fingers. Other styles are the *blusher veil*, which is quite short, only covering the bride's face; the *waltz veil*, also called the *ballerina veil,* which ends at the bride's elbow; the *chapel veil* which is always worn with a floor-length gown and just touches the floor; the *cathedral veil*, the longest of the veils, which trails along behind the bride, being fastened at the shoulders or waist; then, lastly, there is the *mantilla veil,* which is a large circle of solid lace or lace-edged illusion nylon that is worn loosely over the head, like a scarf. This is the style veil that Jackie wore when she married John Kennedy.

A couple of my friends wore their sneakers under their floor-length wedding gowns, just to be comfortable. After all, no one ever sees the bride's shoes anyway. What do you think of that?

I think it's probably a good idea, except the bride's shoes *are* seen off and on during the ceremony and reception.

Depending on the length of the gown, they may be seen as she comes down the aisle on the arm of her father or as she kneels beside the groom at the altar. Then, during the reception there is usually a photo session where the groom removes the bride's garter. Also, sneakers are a little sticky on the dance floor. Some comfortable alternatives are simple ballet slippers, which were my daughter's choice, white satin bedroom slippers or soft, roomy white flats. The main thing to remember is this: Always purchase your wedding shoes a full size larger than you normally wear because your feet will swell during the day, partly from the stress, but especially from being on your feet throughout the reception.

Is there any such thing as an affordable wedding gown? My first time shopping has left me in shock—they're so expensive!

There are several ways to have a beautiful gown without having to spend an outrageous amount. One idea is to borrow a friend's gown, especially if none of your wedding guests has seen it before. Another popular alternative these days is to rent the wedding gown; you'll be amazed to see what a fabulous gown you can rent for less than $300. (By the way, did you know that almost *all* the brides in Japan rent their gowns?) You could have your gown sewn for you, which will save you hundreds of dollars, or purchase a bridemaid's gown in white, which will do the same. When you walk into a bridal salon you usually won't find bridemaids' gowns in white, but if you find one you like, ask if it is available in white. Most of them are. Another idea—my favorite, in fact—is to check out the discount market. There are factory outlets around the country, such as the Gunne Sax outlet in San Francisco and the Jessica McClintock outlet at Woodbury Commons in Central Valley, N.Y., plus there are discount brokers who can order you any name brand gown at up to 40 percent off the retail price. One of the best is the Discount Bridal Service, which is available in all cities nationwide. Then there is the

JCPenney bridal catalog that offers gowns at a tremendous discount. Other discount markets are advertised in a magazine called *Bridal Guide* which is written for the bride on a budget. There are also resale shops here and there throughout the country—you may have a good one near you that will offer a choice of used gowns.

How can I find a reputable bridal salon?

Your best source is word of mouth—talk to other brides who were recently married. Next, ask your bridal coordinator, if you have one, or search out the bridal magazines for names and addresses of stores that carry the lines of dresses advertised. Finally, check with your local Better Business Bureau; if the salon you are considering has had even one complaint, look at it as a big red flag!

I've barely gotten started with the wedding plans and I'm already a nervous wreck! How will I ever make it through seven months' worth of this craziness?

If you're already a nervous wreck, perhaps you're trying to plan a wedding that's too big or too complicated for you to handle. Here are some suggestions:

- Downsize your wedding, including the number of attendants, guests and ceremony participants and the amount of work required to decorate, feed and entertain the guests, etc.
- If you can't downsize, at least delegate as many responsibilities as possible; you may want to turn the whole thing over to a full-service wedding coordinator.
- Don't become obsessed with the wedding plans so that they are all you ever talk about; you'll not only wear yourself out, but your friends and family as well.

- Schedule time for passive and active recreational activities, from strenuous all-day hikes in the mountains to a day at the beach to a Saturday afternoon lunch and a movie.
- Try to relax. Schedule weekly massages, if necessary, and force yourself to *breathe!* Deep breathing is an inexpensive, surefire way to relax. Take long, hot bubble baths or Jacuzzi soaks. Do stretching exercises.

What is a "bridal show"?

A bridal show is an event, often on a Saturday afternoon, where wedding vendors in your area display their wares. Usually, each merchant has a booth that you can visit to get information about the merchant's products or services and there are almost always fashion shows sponsored by area bridal shops. There are also drawings for free goods and services, from honeymoon trips to wedding cakes. You'll want to attend as many of these shows as possible to meet the merchants and get ideas for your wedding, and, who knows, you might even win one of the door prizes.

What about the "something old, something new" tradition?

"Something old, something new, something borrowed, something blue, and a lucky penny in your shoe." The *something old* can be your grandmother's hanky or your family Bible; the *something new* is usually the bride's gown; the *something borrowed* may be a piece of wedding attire borrowed from a happily married friend or relative; the *something blue* is usually a blue garter; and, of course, the lucky penny is worn in your shoe.

What is a "removable skirt"?

There is a trend toward a bridal gown that has a removable long skirt, leaving a shorter (sometimes *quite* short and sexy) skirt underneath, more suitable for dancing at the reception.

What is "bustling"?

This is the alternative to the removable skirt—another convenient way to dance in your wedding gown. The train of the wedding gown is pulled up in back and attached at the waist with buttons, hooks or ribbons, creating an attractive, natural-looking bustle. This gets the train up off the floor so that it doesn't get stepped on while the bride is walking or dancing.

What about my makeup for my wedding day? Shouldn't it be a little exaggerated because of the photography and all?

Yes, but be careful. There was one wedding I attended where the bride hired a professional makeup artist who overdid it to the point where the bride didn't even look like herself. In fact, I was embarrassed for her because she came down the aisle smiling radiantly on her father's arm, obviously confident and pleased with the way she looked when in actuality she was so overdone she almost looked like a clown. Take it easy: Add a little extra eyeliner and eye shadow and a darker shade of lipstick, but be very careful with the rest of your face. The biggest mistake I see is *way* too much blusher!

I would like to have my bridal gown preserved. How do I go about it?

The first step is to be sure your gown is cleaned as soon as possible after your wedding day. The tendency is that, once you've survived the big day and gone off on your honeymoon, the wedding gown loses all its "Cinderella preciousness" and is left hanging folded over a hanger in Mom's closet for weeks, or even months. What should happen is this: Have someone, probably your mother, take your gown to the dry cleaners as soon as possible after the wedding. That way, any spots, perspiration stains and dirt can be attacked while they are still relatively fresh. Then, once cleaned, the gown should be stored in an acid-free box with acid-free tissues.

I have a lot of fears about my wedding day, but one of the worst is that everything will run behind schedule and the guests will sit waiting and waiting for the ceremony to begin. What do I do if this happens?

Don't panic if you fall behind schedule—the ceremony will wait for you. I've attended dozens of weddings that ran late and they weren't disastrous. We just sat and soaked up the ambiance and the lovely music. Try to remain flexible and calm—and remember to smile! It's *your* day, and we'll all wait on you—don't worry!

What's the worst thing you've ever seen happen to the bride on her wedding day?

There was one bride who broke her leg on a ski weekend with her fiance three days before the wedding (how she had time to go off on a holiday so close to the wedding, I can't imagine) and one of the local florists tried to cheer her by decorating her crutches with white satin and fresh flowers. What seemed a disaster at the time had a happy ending, and what great wedding photos! Another bride was so nervous she forgot *all* her underthings, plus her wedding shoes. One of her bridesmaids offered her a spare pair of white heels, but, alas, there were no extra "frillies" to be had, so she walked down the aisle bare-legged, and did anyone know or care? Of course, not! So, don't worry about anything—if the unexpected should happen, just smile and enjoy your day in spite of it. As long as you and your fiance finish up the day as husband and wife, how little it all matters anyway. Don't you agree?

Chapter 8

The Groom

Some of my friends want to give me a bachelor party, but I feel awkward about this because this is my second marriage and, basically, it's the same group of guys who already threw a bachelor party for me once before. Should I say, "Thanks, but no thanks?"

Absolutely not! You're not married at the moment, so you're very much a bachelor and deserving of a night out with the boys. Although this traditional party originated as a gathering together of all the groom's friends as a sort of "goodbye to your bachelor days," it has evolved into a fun time where all the men involved can get together before the wedding, including your friends, members of your wedding party, father and brothers. Let your friends make the plans, and then...enjoy!

How do I choose my groomsmen and ushers?

Choose your groomsmen from among your brothers, the bride's brothers, your cousins or your best friends. You can even choose your father to be your best man, if you like. Your groomsmen may also double as ushers, or you may have both groomsmen and ushers, in which case you will need one usher for every 50 guests. If you do decide to have your groomsmen double as ushers, this is fine except that you may want to have at least one actual usher to be on hand near the back of the church to seat any last minute arrivals as you and your groomsmen are assembling in the side room in preparation for the processional to begin.

It seems that at every wedding I've attended lately, whether the wedding is during the day or evening, the men wear tuxes. Is this always necessary?

Actually, formal wear is only required for a formal or semi-formal wedding, or a wedding after 5 p.m. Otherwise, you may wear a dark suit or, if it is a summer wedding, a linen jacket over dark slacks or a navy jacket over white slacks. For a very formal wedding you may be required to wear a cutaway coat with striped trousers or a black tailcoat with black trousers. One popular trend is to wear navy blazers with white trousers (works well for an outdoor wedding). Most men already have these hanging in their closets, but if they need to purchase them, they will be practical additions to any man's wardrobe that can be worn again and again. By the way, most stores offer a *groom's special* whereby the groom gets his tux rental for free if all the groomsmen order their tuxes from the same store.

Would it be worth it to purchase a tuxedo?

Many grooms think it is a wise investment to purchase a tuxedo. If you are considering this, be sure it is a classic black, one-button, single-breasted one that won't tend to go out of style.

What is a "collar extender"? I've never seen one.

A collar extender is an ingenious little loop of elastic that can add an inch or so to the size of your shirt collar by extending the space between the button and buttonhole.

Our wedding is going to be a "very formal evening" affair, which evidently requires full-dress tail coats and trousers. My fiancee wants me to wear a black top hat and white gloves as well. I can handle the white gloves, but I'm just not the type of guy to wear a black top hat. I'm afraid I'll feel like a chimney sweep!

You're in luck! The black top hat and white gloves are *optional* for a very formal evening wedding; however, if you eliminate the top hat, forget the white gloves as well.

I had no idea that planning a wedding could be so complicated and exhausting. I feel sorry for my fiancee because she's working about 10 hours a day at the office and then trying to make calls and meet with caterers on the weekend. She's on edge all the time. How can I help her cope with the anxiety of it?

Look in Chapter 7 for the advice I gave a bride who found herself in this same predicament. You may want to have a talk with your fiancee and seriously consider downsizing the wedding and reception, or you may be able to help her delegate some of the responsibilities or, preferably, help her with some of them yourself. For example, you can do some calling on your own, getting quotes from caterers, dance bands or photographers, and when it comes to relaxation and recreation, you can be the one to insist that you "run away from home" once in a while. Meanwhile, you both need to lighten up and keep the big picture in mind: Your object is to become man and wife and when you sink into your wedding bed at the end of the big day, as long as that has been accomplished, a couple little snafus won't matter at all. Trust me—you'll see!

How soon do I need to reserve the tuxes for the wedding? My fiancee said that they should be reserved as soon as she buys her wedding dress.

Fortunately, rental tuxes aren't usually in short supply, so this is one of the few things that can wait until two or three months before the wedding.

Is there some way to save money on the tux rental?

There are several ways, in fact. First, avoid the top-of-the-line name brands; go for the lesser-known tuxedo companies. Second, look for a discount rental shop where tuxedos rent for about 20 percent less than the full-service retail stores. Finally, look for a package deal (the "rent four, get the groom's tux for free" deal).

Is it all right if I take off my tuxedo jacket during the reception?

Actually, it has become quite popular for the groom to have two looks, one for the ceremony and one for the reception. By removing your jacket for the reception and replacing it with a colorful vest and tie, you'll accomplish this feat and be much more comfortable, as well.

What are some of things I should be doing in preparation for our wedding?

Oh, you'll be busy! Here are some of your responsibilities:

- Order and pay for your bride's wedding ring.
- Help make out the guest list.
- Select your groomsmen and ushers.
- Plan your honeymoon and update your passport, arrange for visas, international driver's license and inoculations, if necessary.
- Visit stores with your fiancee to establish wedding gift registries.
- Arrange to pay for your bride's bouquet, mothers' corsages and boutonnieres for the men.
- Help your parents plan the rehearsal dinner.
- Give or attend a bachelor party.
- Help your fiancee write thank-you notes (the more you get done ahead of time, the less you'll have to write after the honeymoon).
- Put the clergyman's or judge's fee in a sealed envelope and give it to the best man, who will deliver it before or after the ceremony.
- Make any necessary arrangements for transportation, including your getaway vehicle.
- Make any necessary arrangements for travel and lodging for your groomsmen and ushers.

- Purchase or make reservations to rent the wedding attire for you and the men in your wedding party.
- If asked, help your fiancee choose your ceremony and reception sites, the musicians and musical selections, etc.
- Take your fiancee to meet with your clergyman, including premarital counseling sessions, if required.
- Put your financial affairs in order, including making changes in your insurance policies and checking accounts.
- Buy thank-you gifts for your best man, groomsmen, ring bearer, ushers and others who will help with your wedding.
- Select and purchase a gift for your bride, if you are giving her something special in addition to her wedding ring.
- Make a date with your fiancee for blood tests and picking up your marriage license.
- Make arrangements to move your belongings into your new apartment or home.
- Pack for your honeymoon.
- Purchase traveler's checks.
- Keep track of your marriage license and be *sure* to bring it with you to the ceremony!

Do you have any creative ideas for a bachelor party?

Planning something active seems to be popular these days, from a bicycle marathon, to a golf tournament (complete with trophies), to a camping or backpacking weekend, to a racquetball tournament, to a night out at a ball game. Actually, the more physical the better because a lot of stress builds up in the months before a wedding and you could all stand to blow off a little steam!

Chapter 9

The Bride's Attendants

I have been a bridal attendant or maid of honor in several weddings over the past two years. Am I obligated to return this honor by asking each of these brides to be an attendant in my wedding?

Absolutely not! After you've decided how many attendants you're going to have, make your selections from your heart, including those friends or family members closest to you, whether you were included in their weddings or not. Honor the rest of your friends in other ways: as candlelighters, guest book attendant, hostess, etc. Remember that your wedding day is a uniquely special day in your life, not an occasion for returning social obligations.

What is a "snowball wedding"?

This is a wedding where all your bridal attendants wear white and the men usually wear white dinner jackets and black trousers. Sometimes the mothers wear white as well. The only color in the wedding is that of the flowers, which should be bright and vibrant. If you decide to have a snowball wedding, here is one word of caution: Be sure all the whites match. If your gown is slightly creamy, for example, it will look dirty next to your attendants' blue-white gowns. Select your gown first and use a fabric swatch to go shopping for everyone else.

What is a "bridesmaids' luncheon"?

It is a luncheon that is usually held a week or so before the wedding; it may be hosted by the bride for her bridesmaids, or vice versa. This is a good time for the bride to present her attendants with her gifts to them, especially if the gift is a piece of jewelry or clothing that will be worn during the wedding, such as a pearl necklace or pair of gloves. Also, the bridesmaids may use this opportunity to present the bride with their joint gift.

Do my bridesmaids' gowns have to be the same style as my wedding gown?

No, that isn't imperative, although it is normally the case. For example, if your dress is a full, hooped "Southern-Belle" styled gown, the bridesmaids would look pretty silly wearing clingy, sophisticated 90s gowns.

What about my flower girl? Is it all right if she wears white?

Yes, but be sure the white of her dress matches the white of your gown. If you *can* match the whites, there is nothing quite as adorable as a short white dress tied in back with a wide bow in the same color or fabric as your bridesmaids' gowns. Another possibility is for your flower girl to wear a short little girl's version of the bridesmaids' gowns.

How can I be sure the sizing is correct for my bridesmaids' dresses?

Be aware that if you're ordering gowns from a bridal salon, the sizing is different than if you're ordering regular ready-to-wear. The bridal salon attire will probably run smaller, which means that if a woman normally wears a size 12, she will need a size 14. This sizing usually holds true for the bride, as well.

I would like my bridesmaids to be able to wear their dresses after the wedding. What do you suggest?

Try shopping in the "After Five" or "Special Occasion" section of your local department store; you'll find a large selection of dresses that will do double-duty and you'll be happy your bridesmaids' hard-earned money can be spent on dresses they can wear again.

Chapter 10

The Groom's Attendants

What are the duties of the "groomsmen"?

When a man agrees to participate in a wedding, he takes on a number of responsibilities. The best man has most of the duties. First of all, he helps the groom select a rental store for the men's attire; then he follows through to see that alterations are made and the clothes are picked up or delivered in time; he also confirms any other orders the groom has made; he helps the groom dress; he takes full charge of the marriage license, clergyman's fee, the bride's wedding ring, the groom's passport, airline tickets, wallet, keys and honeymoon hotel confirmations; he signs the marriage license; he proposes the first toast at the reception; he dances with the bride, her mother and each of the bridesmaids; he places the couple's going-away luggage in their getaway vehicle; and after the wedding, he returns all the men's rented wedding attire. Whew!

The rest of the groomsmen have it made, compared to the best man. All they have to do is look handsome and dance with the bride, mothers and bridesmaids at the reception, plus help the best man with any last-minute details.

Three of my groomsmen live in other states. How can I be sure all the men's tuxes are sized the same?

This can be a big problem because there will be several tailors involved. Here are a few guidelines for you to pass on to each of the men:

- The jackets should fit snugly, but with no arm bulges, and there should be a little room at the waist.
- The jacket sleeves should end at the men's wrist bones.
- The trousers should touch the top of the shoes with enough slack so the crease breaks slightly.
- The shirt collars should be tight enough to hug the neck, but not so tight that the lapels buckle.

Who decides what the groomsmen will wear?

The groomsmen's attire is dictated by the formality of the wedding and it should coordinate with the groom's attire.

Does the color of the cummerbunds and bow ties have to match the color of the bridesmaids' gowns?

Usually they do, but the latest trend is to have cummerbunds and bow ties made from the exact same fabric as their dresses, even if the fabric is a print or stripe.

I've heard the terms "groomsmen" and "ushers" interchanged. Is there a difference?

Yes and no. If the men who stand beside the groom during the ceremony as his groomsmen also serve as ushers beforehand, the term is interchangeable. However, if there are two separate groups of men, one who stands beside the groom during the ceremony and one who ushers the guests to their seats, in that particular wedding the terms are not interchangeable. Confusing, isn't it?

Chapter 11

The Couple's Parents

Is there some rule about which mother contacts the other mother first, once the engagement has been announced?

The groom's mother should call the bride's mother first, telling her how happy she and her husband are about the engagement and making arrangements for them to meet the bride's parents. If for some reason the groom's mother doesn't call after a reasonable amount of time, and she may not understand that she should, it is fine for the bride's mother to place the first call.

I have a problem that is probably pretty common these days: I have two fathers, my real father and my stepfather. I am close to both of them, although I don't see my real father very often since my mother remarried 10 years ago. Which once should I have give me away? I love them both and I don't want to hurt either one of their feelings.

You're right—this is definitely not a new question. There are several things you can do. If this is an emotionally wrenching problem for you and it's putting a damper on your wedding plans, for your sake, my first preference is that you walk down the aisle alone. Second best would be for your natural father to give you away, but include your stepfather in the ceremony in some meaningful way, such as having him read a poem or portion of scripture you have selected. In the case where there are children from a previous marriage, it works very well to be escorted down the aisle by one or two of the children (whether boys or girls).

Should our mothers wear the same length and style of dress?

It's a good idea if their dresses or gowns are similar in style and length, although they shouldn't be the same color. Also, they should not wear the same color as the bridesmaids, nor should they wear white, unless, of course, it is a *snowball wedding* where everyone wears white. The bride's mother has the responsibility of selecting her dress first, then notifying the groom's mother of her choice. If the two families live close to each other it is very nice if the two mothers can get together so the groom's mother can see her dress. If the families don't live close, a photo can be sent along with a description and fabric sample of the dress. By the way, the mothers' gowns should never be floor-length unless the bride's gown is also.

My parents divorced years ago and have never remarried. Where should they be seated during the ceremony?

You would think that after your father gives you away they could be seated next to each other on the same pew, but according to wedding etiquette, this is usually not done. Your mother should sit in the first pew along with her parents; your father should sit in the pew behind your mother, alongside his parents.

My father is really nervous about walking me down the aisle. Is it necessary for him to do that slow, hesitation step?

The *hesitation step* is almost never used today, which should be a relief to your father. All he needs to do is hold his head high and walk slowly and naturally. It will help a lot if you practice with him at home off and on before the wedding. By the way, it's a rare father who isn't nervous about giving his daughter away.

Unfortunately, my parents have recently gone through a bitter divorce; in fact, as of the moment they aren't even speaking to each other. How do I handle this problem at my wedding?

First of all, I hope they have the maturity to be civil and pleasant for your sake. However, there are several things you can do to alleviate this sticky situation. During the ceremony have your mother seated in the first row; then, after your father has given you away, he should be seated *two* rows in back of your mother. During the reception, forgo the receiving line so they don't have to stand together. Then, by using place cards, arrange the table seating so that your mother and father are at least two tables apart. Your mother will probably sit with the groom's parents, the clergyman and his or her spouse. Seat your father with other family members, perhaps his parents or brothers and sisters. Remember, this is *their* problem—not yours! So, keep smiling no matter what and enjoy your day.

What should the two fathers wear to the wedding?

The bride's father usually wears the same attire as the groomsmen, which is dictated by the formality of the wedding and which should coordinate with the groom's attire. The groom's father has the choice of wearing the same attire as the bride's father or wearing a dark suit.

Chapter 12

Themes and Decorations

I'm not a very creative person and I'm having trouble coming up with a theme for our wedding and reception. Is it absolutely necessary to have some sort of theme?

No, it's not necessary, but it will actually make your wedding and reception easier to plan. There are many theme ideas, but if your family happens to have a strong ethnic background, why not go with a cultural theme? This is one of the easiest solutions to your problem. Wear wedding attire that reflects your country's origin; include foods, music and favors that follow your ethnic theme. Your wedding colors can be determined by those in your country's flag; for example, if you're Swedish, your colors would be blue and yellow. You can even add small flags to your floral arrangements. Best of all, include as many traditional customs as possible (visit your local library to do your research). By using an ethnic theme, your wedding will plan itself, although your guests will think you're *especially* creative!

My fiance and I are both of Mexican descent, and we like the idea of an ethnic theme; if we were to have a Mexican theme for our wedding, what are some ideas we could include?

Why not take your cues from Mexico itself—strive for a wedding as ethnically authentic as possible.

Here are some Mexican wedding traditions:

- The entire ceremony is in Spanish, of course.
- A Catholic wedding mass is held at 9 p.m.
- The church is decorated with white roses.
- Guests sit wherever they please (not on the bride's or groom's side).
- The bride's only attendants are her four godmothers, each responsible for one aspect of the ceremony: One makes three bouquets (one for the bride to lay on the altar, one to keep and one to toss at the reception); another godmother carries a dish with 13 gold arras (coins) along with the couple's rings; the other two godmothers are responsible to carry a rope with a cross they drape in a figure 8 around the couple as the couple kneels at the altar, uniting them.
- The couple sits at a small table by themselves at the reception.
- All the single women perform a line dance called "La Vibora" (*the snake*).
- The reception usually goes on all night.

What about some other theme ideas?

Here are five theme suggestions for you to consider:

Snowball

This is a wedding where everyone wears white, including the mothers and grandmothers. Be sure all the whites are the same.

Black and white

All the wedding costumes are black and white. The men may wear black tuxes, the attendants black gowns with white trim, the flower girl wears white and the ring bearer wears black. This is a very popular 90s theme, but be sure there is a little color splashed around somewhere, in the flowers and ribbons, for example, or the wedding will lose its festive feeling of celebration.

Wreaths

Decorate various sizes of Styrofoam or grapevine wreaths and hang them on the pews and pillars. Also, oversized wreaths work well when hung on the walls in the front of the ceremony site.

Christmas

This is an easy theme to work with because of the Christmas trees, holly, poinsettias, candles and evergreenery available during December. Also, trail strands of tiny Christmas tree lights over and around the decorations for a special touch of winter wonderland.

Victorian

A Victorian theme needs plenty of lace, ribbon, hearts and trailing ribbon. Also, the bride and her attendants may want to wear bustled gowns and high-buttoned shoes.

I think I like the idea of a Victorian wedding, especially since I will be wearing my grandmother's old-fashioned lace gown. What are some other things we can incorporate?

In addition to the ideas mentioned in the Victorian section, you may want to carry a tussy mussy (a small cluster of flowers tied with ribbon or inserted into an elegant cone-shaped holder), and add lace or ribbon to your bridesmaids' headpieces, to the floral pew markers and the reception centerpieces. Another Victorian custom is to incorporate rose petals into the ceremony and reception: Fill a delicate basket for your flower girl to scatter down the aisle; strew them along the center of the reception tables and on the cake table; and set fragrant baskets full alongside your guest book. Candles also add a romantic Victorian touch, especially for an evening wedding, and, finally, you may want to consider placing a single rosebud tied with a lace ribbon at every female guest's place setting.

I want the center aisle to be decorated in some really dramatic way, instead of the usual pew bows. Do you have any ideas?

Well, in addition to the opulent floral sprays mentioned in Chapter 17, you may want to consider adding 6-foot pew candlesticks every other pew, decorated profusely with ribbon, tulle netting, trailing silk or live ivy and any silk or live flowers of your choice. These candlesticks can be rented from some florists and most wedding rental stores. Another trick is to stand a tall topiary tree beside every pew, decorated with trailing ribbons and tiny silk rosebuds. You can also create a striking ambiance by draping the pews together with floral or evergreen garlands, wide fabric ribbons or swirls of gracefully twisted tulle netting.

What is a "chuppah"?

It is a canopy that is held over the heads of the bride and groom and their two honor attendants during a traditional Jewish ceremony. It may be a stationary structure and is sometimes made of flowers, but it is usually decorated with elegantly decorated cloth. If it is large enough, the parents may stand under the chuppah as well. The chuppah is a symbol of the earliest rites of Hebrew marriage when the chief purpose of the marriage was the propagation of the human race and the ceremony took place in the presence of witnesses in the bridal chamber. Later, when this became objectionable, a tent was substituted to symbolize the bridal chamber, and then, eventually, a scarf or canopy became the custom.

I'm going to be married at home in our combination living room/dining room, in front of the fireplace. What can we do to decorate without overdoing it?

The nice thing about a home wedding is that the natural charm and intimacy of the home itself offers a romantic ambiance for the wedding; also, a home setting takes very little in the way of decorations. The first step is to unclutter the rooms; remove a few of the oversized pieces of furniture and clear away at least half of the knickknacks, family photos, etc. This will leave room for white folding chairs, if you choose to use them, and a few flower arrangements. The fireplace mantle can be decorated with greens, flowers, candles and ribbons. An altar can be made up quite easily by covering any small table with a lace or damask tablecloth and you can borrow a kneeling bench from your church or rent one from a wedding rental store. If white wooden folding chairs are set in the middle of the room, it is nice to drape the chairs with ribbon and flowers to create a center aisle. If the room is too small for extra chairs, however, it is perfectly fine for the guests to stand during the ceremony.

I always wanted to have a garden wedding, but we're getting married indoors in January. How can I create a garden setting?

Depending on any religious restrictions, you might consider bringing in white wrought iron benches, trellises, white wooden arbors and picket fencing. Then add colorful flowering potted plants, shrubs and trees (even silk ones). This same idea works, by the way, for converting a homely reception hall into a charming, blooming garden.

Speaking of homely reception halls, we're being stuck with a school gymnasium, of all things, which happens to be the only building in our small town large enough to hold all our guests. Help! What can we do?

Borrow some of the same tricks high school students use when converting a plain school gym into a romantic wonderland for their senior prom. First, they fill the room with all the silk ficus trees and potted shrubs they can find. Then they wrap hundreds of tiny white Christmas tree lights around these trees and plants, over the windows and doorways and along the stage and railings. Finally, they fill hundreds of balloons with helium and suspend them from the ceiling with curled lengths of crinkle-tie ribbon. By using these few inexpensive props they are able to create a warm ambiance for their party, especially once the sun goes down and the overheads are turned off, leaving only the sparkle and glow of the tiny white lights.

Another solution is to fill the homely place with candles, more expensive than borrowed Christmas tree lights, but very effective. Also, you can break up the monotony of the room by arranging clusters of plants and trees here and there across the floor.

Chapter 13

The Rehearsal

Is it always necessary to have a formal rehearsal? We have several members of the wedding party who will barely make it here for the day of the wedding, much less for a rehearsal the night before.

Will you have music? Will you walk down the aisle? Are there bridesmaids? Unless you're having a *very* simple or a *very* informal wedding, you definitely need a rehearsal, even if it has to be a few hours before the ceremony. Believe me, I have seen couples who thought they could get by without it, and they were *always* sorry. A wedding is composed of many parts, all of which must fit together like a puzzle; for example, the ushers need to be briefed; the organist and other musicians need to rehearse, including the pace of the processional; everyone involved needs to walk through the sequence of the ceremony, especially the bride and groom who have the most important part.

When is the rehearsal usually held?

It is common to hold the rehearsal on the evening before the wedding at a time that is most convenient for the clergyman and also that allows time for the rehearsal dinner to follow.

Who supervises the ceremony rehearsal itself?

Usually the clergyman, but if not, appoint someone knowledgeable, such as a wedding coordinator.

How long does a wedding rehearsal usually last?

If the officiant takes charge and gets things moving, an hour and a half should be more than enough time to run through the entire service twice, which is ideal.

What should we bring to the rehearsal?

Bring several "pretend" bouquets for the bride and bridesmaids to practice with (make them ahead of time out of ribbons left over from engagement parties, bridal showers or wedding gifts that have already been opened). Bring the marriage license to give to the clergyman for safekeeping. Bring and deliver checks for those who are being paid to participate, such as the soloists, organist, harpist, etc. The bride and groom should bring their gifts for their attendants and groomsmen, if they haven't already given these gifts on a previous occasion.

Does the bride actually take part in the rehearsal? Isn't it proper for someone to stand in for her while she sits and listens?

That used to be the case. In the 90s, however, it is perfectly acceptable and preferred, in fact, for the bride to go through the motions, along with the groom and the rest of the wedding party. The bride, her father and her attendants especially need to practice walking down the aisle. Once everyone is settled in place in the front of the church or synagogue, the rabbi, priest or minister will explain the sequence of the service, but won't use the words of the actual marriage ceremony itself. Instead he will say, "At this point, you will recite your vows to each other," etc.

Who is usually invited to the rehearsal dinner?

Believe it or not, here we go again with another pesky guest list. It is really important that everyone be invited who should be invited; this is no time for hurt feelings. To begin with, all of the attendants and their spouses or fiances are invited, along with the parents of any children who are participating in the wedding (the children, if very young, should be left with a baby sitter during the dinner), the clergyman and his or her spouse, special out-of-town relatives, including the grandparents, the parents of the couple and, *of course,* the honored guests, the bride and groom.

Who normally hosts the rehearsal dinner?

Actually, anyone may host it, but it is traditionally hosted by the groom's parents. It may also be hosted by the bride's parents, bride's or groom's grandparents or other relatives, or any member of the wedding party. It doesn't have to be a formal affair, by the way.

Is there a traditional order of events for a rehearsal dinner?

Other than the toasts, which are traditionally a part of any rehearsal dinner celebration, there are no rules to follow. Here are few things, however, that you may want to include during the evening:

- See that introductions are made all around; this is a wonderful opportunity for the extended families of the bride and groom to meet and get to know each other.

- Various family members may want to tell little stories about the bride or groom when they were young.

- Home videos or slide shows are fun, showing the couple as they were growing up. (Be sure you have a supply of tissues on hand, especially close by the mothers of the bride and groom!)

- If the get-together is quite informal, you may include swimming, karaoke singing, mixer games, volleyball or horseshoes—anything to loosen everyone up after all the stress of planning the wedding.

- This is also a great time to say "thank-you" to all those present who have helped with the wedding preparations and to give gifts to members of your wedding party, if you haven't already done so.

The important thing to remember when planning the rehearsal dinner is for it to have a comfortable setting where everyone can relax, get to know each other and enjoy each other before the big day.

What toasts are normally given during the rehearsal dinner?

This is the usual order of toasts:

- The best man toasts the bride and groom.
- The groom toasts his bride and her parents.
- The bride toasts her groom and his parents.

Following these traditional toasts, anyone may offer one and, by the way, all these toasts are usually more personal and humorous than those at the wedding reception.

Chapter 14

The Ceremony

What are the most popular ceremony sites?

The most popular sites in the 90s are traditional religious sites, such as a church, chapel, temple or cathedral. Then, there is the bride's home, a hall, a private club, hotel ball room, restaurant or a judge's chambers, if it is a simple civil ceremony. However, when it comes to the nontraditional, the sky's *literally* the limit, when you consider being married in a hot air balloon, at the top of a ski slope, on the bank of a river or lake, beside a waterfall, on a cruise ship or on a Hawaiian beach at sunset. You name it—you can probably be married *on* it, *in* it or *beside* it! It's interesting that with the success of the book and movie titled *The Bridges of Madison County*, at least 30 couples have wed on Madison County's covered bridges in the past year.

We're going to be married in a church that has three sections with two center aisles, instead of one traditional center aisle dividing two sections. We expect to have about 150 guests—how can they be seated so they aren't all spread out?

The best way is to ribbon off one of the side sections, preferably the left section, and then use the left aisle for the processional and the right aisle for the recessional; another solution is to use the right aisle for both the processional and recessional, as if it were the only aisle in the church.

We plan to have a very simple, brief civil ceremony in a small but attractive room in our county courthouse. Will it be all right if I wear a floor-length wedding gown? We're going from there directly to a large hotel reception, and I want to be wearing my gown when I arrive.

You definitely have a problem here because you don't normally wear traditional wedding attire when being married in a municipal building by a judge or justice of the peace. I'm sure you can find a lovely afternoon dress or suit that would work for both locations. Another solution would be to ask the justice of the peace to perform the ceremony in front of the guests at the hotel; that way, you can wear anything you'd like and everyone will enjoy seeing the wedding take place.

What kind of official is authorized to perform marriages in a civil ceremony?

Depending on your state, a judge, a justice of the peace, a mayor, a county clerk or, perhaps, a notary public, depending on your state's regulations. Call your local marriage license bureau to ask for references.

What are the other ways a civil ceremony differs from other wedding ceremonies?

Usually a civil ceremony is small and nonreligious; it can be performed in a courthouse or a judge's chambers, of course, but may also be performed at any other nonreligious location, such as a restaurant, country club or at your home. The bride and groom usually only have one attendant each. The reception that follows may be small, immediately following the ceremony, or large and lavish, planned for later in the day at another location.

I'd like to be married at home, but I don't want my parents to go through anything like in *Father of the Bride*. How can we make it special without going overboard?

A home wedding is one of my favorites because of the charm of the setting. In order to keep things simple, think about some of these suggestions: Move out any really cumbersome furniture to leave room for white folding chairs to be used by the parents, grandparents and any elderly guests—everyone else stands during the ceremony; limit your attendants to one each—a maid or matron of honor and the best man; keep the music simple—a string quartet, single harpist or even recorded music is fine; select a wedding gown with no train (a train takes up too much room). Of course, if the wedding takes place in the garden of the home, and the garden is quite large, you may have room for more attendants and musicians, as well as a dance floor that can be rented and set up on top of the lawn. Don't forget to decorate your old childhood swing!

What is an "arch-of-steel" ceremony?

The *arch of steel* is very simply the raising of the blades of military swords or sabers at the end of a military wedding, creating an arch for the bride and groom to pass under. The only groomsmen who participate in this ceremony, of course, are those wearing their military uniforms; any civilian groomsmen may stand alongside with their hands at their side during the arching of the weapons. This arch-of-steel ceremony is the main distinction of a military wedding. Then, at the reception, the groom's sword or saber is used to cut the first piece of wedding cake. Both of these delightful customs make for wonderful photo ops!

We definitely want to be married in our family church which has a large sanctuary that seats more than 800 people, but we only expect to have 200 guests. How can we keep the service intimate and personal?

There are a couple of things you can do. The first is the most important: Block off the back of the church by swagging ribbon, tulle netting or evergreen garlands across all the pews you won't be using; this will force your guests to sit toward the front of the church. Next, by placing rows of silk ficus trees or live potted plants in front of the pews you don't need, you create the illusion of a small, cozy chapel.

I've been to two weddings in the past year where someone in the wedding party fainted. I don't want this to happen at my wedding; what can be done to prevent this?

I can't count the times I've seen this happen! There are some precautions that can be taken, however. The first is to be sure there is plenty of ventilation, even if you need to add floor fans on each side of the wedding party. The next thing is to teach the members of the wedding party how to stand: They should never lock their knees and they should shift their weight from one foot to the other. The best suggestion of all is to keep smelling salts close by. If, after all of this, someone does start to faint, have the person sit down and put his or her head between his or her knees.

What are some things we should know before my fiance and I decide which church we want to be married in?

Whatever you do, don't reserve a church until you know all its rules, some of which may restrict the plans you had for your wedding. Here are some of the questions you should ask:

- Is the church available for the day and time you prefer?
- What are the restrictions for flowers? Music? Photography? Videography? Candles? Dress? Decorations?
- Are you required to be married by one of the church's ministers? Or may you have another minister marry you in that church?
- Are you required to pay a fee to the organist, custodian, etc.?
- What is the fee for the use of the church? For how many hours?

- Are there restrictions on what may be tossed at the bride and groom after the ceremony (such as rice or bird seed)?
- Will you be allowed to erect a canopy, use an aisle runner, etc.?
- Are there dressing rooms for the bridal party?
- Will you and the florist have access to the church in plenty of time before the service in order to decorate?
- If you will be required to use their minister, will counseling be required? And are there requirements as to your beliefs and religious backgrounds?
- Will you be allowed to write your own vows, if that is what you would like to do? Or will you be required to comply with their traditional wording?
- Are you allowed to use your own original readings, or are there religious restrictions?
- What ceremony accessories will they provide, such as an aisle runner, candelabra or chuppah?
- Will you be required to use and pay for the services of their wedding coordinator?

Note of advice: Get it all in writing!

Have you ever heard of having two wedding ceremonies? One civil and one religious?

Yes. In fact, this is more common than you would think. The civil ceremony is first, followed by the religious ceremony. If the two ceremonies are several weeks or months apart, the second ceremony is usually more of a re-enactment. For example, the clergyman may say, "Do you *acknowledge* this woman?" rather than *take*. Also, during the second ceremony the bride is usually not "given away" by her father and she wouldn't wear symbols of virginity, such as a bridal veil, orange blossoms or a myrtle wreath.

Otherwise, the ceremony and reception may be as elaborate and festive as you would like.

A recent example of a civil ceremony followed by a religious ceremony is the case of Heather Locklear (star of *Melrose Place)* who married Richie Sambora (Bon Jovi guitarist). First they were married in a civil ceremony in Sambora's New Jersey home; two days later they married in Paris in a lavish Episcopal wedding at the American Cathedral.

What is a memorial candle?

A memorial candle is a candle that usually stands off to the side of the altar area during the ceremony. It is lit in memory of a loved one who has passed away during the year preceding the wedding. It is a very nice tribute that is usually mentioned in the ceremony program, as well.

We're having a Protestant service; can you give me an idea of the timetable leading up to the ceremony?

First of all, if the photographer plans to take formal shots before the ceremony, you and the rest of the wedding party will need to be ready two hours before the ceremony. Following the photo session, this is a typical timetable:

- 45 minutes before the ceremony: The ushers receive last minute instructions for seating the guests, locate the ceremony programs and gather at the doors that lead into the ceremony site.
- 30 minutes before the ceremony: The organist and/or other musicians begin to play the prelude while the ushers escort guests to their seats.
- 20 minutes before the ceremony: The groom, the best man and the groomsmen meet in a side room with the clergyman, unless all the groomsmen are serving as ushers, in which case they arrive right before the processional begins. The clergyman will ask to see the marriage license at this time, and the best man may deliver the clergyman's fee, if this wasn't taken care of previously.

- 10 minutes before the ceremony: The parents and grandparents of the groom and the grandparents and mother of the bride assemble in the vestibule, ready to be escorted to their seats by an usher.

- Five minutes before the ceremony: The grandparents are escorted to their seats.

- Four minutes before the ceremony: The groom's mother is escorted to her seat, followed by the groom's father walking a few feet behind.

- Three minutes before the ceremony: The bride's mother is escorted to her seat while the bride, her father, her attendants and the ring bearer line up in the vestibule in preparation for the processional.

- Two minutes before the ceremony: Two of the ushers walk together side by side to the front of the aisle to unroll the aisle runner, if one is used.

- One minute before the wedding: The ushers, if also serving as groomsmen, then hurry out a side entrance to join the groom, clergyman and other groomsmen who are waiting together. If not serving as groomsmen, they wait in the vestibule after unrolling the aisle runner, ready to lead the processional down the aisle.

- Ceremony time: The groom, his groomsmen and the clergyman enter and stand in front of the ceremony site. All eyes turn to watch the processional.

Please don't be surprised if this schedule doesn't go quite as planned. All that matters is that you, the beautiful bride, eventually make it down the aisle. The guests aren't checking their watches—they're just enjoying the celebration!

What are "bell ringers"?

They are young boys or girls who walk up and down the aisles of the church ringing delicate clear glass bells (such

as a crystal dinner bell), thus announcing the official beginning of the wedding ceremony. At a recent wedding I
attended, two 5-year-old girls served as bell ringers, walking slowly down the side aisles from the rear of the church
(as they gently rang their bells) and then joining in the
front of the church, holding hands and walking together
back down the center aisle. This is definitely an effective
and adorable way to get the guests' attention; it is also a
tactful way to include more children in the ceremony, just
in case you happen to have more "applicants" than
"positions available," which is true with so many brides.

**I've been to so many weddings where the first few
bridesmaids try to do the "hesitation step," followed by
the rest of the bridal attendants who just walk down
the aisle normally. How can we avoid this?**

The hesitation step, which is when there is a distinct pause
between each step, is really quite an old-fashioned tradition and isn't necessary. Instead, have your bridal attendants walk slowly, keeping three to four pews' distance between them.

**What is the actual order of the procession as we come
down the aisle?**

It depends on what type of service. For most Protestant
services, this is the order:

- The ushers (walking in pairs, the shortest of them
  leading).
- The bridesmaids (walking individually or in
  pairs).
- The honor attendant (always walking alone).
- The ring bearer.
- The flower girl(s).
- The bride and the bride's father (walking
  together, the bride on her father's right arm).
- Pages or train bearers, if any (walking behind the
  bride carrying the train of her gown).

For Catholic services, the processional, which is optional, is usually in the same order.

Jewish processionals vary according to local custom and the preferences of the family, but in the simplest ceremonies, this is the usual order:

- The bride's grandparents (walking side by side, her grandmother on her grandfather's right).
- The groom's grandparents (also walking side by side, his grandmother on his grandfather's right).
- The ushers (walking in pairs).
- The best man (walking alone).
- The groom and his parents (walking side by side with his father in the center, the groom on his father's left and his mother on his father's right).
- The bridesmaids (walking in pairs).
- The honor attendant (walking alone).
- The flower girl (walking alone).
- The bride and her parents (walking side by side with the bride in the center, her father holding her left arm and her mother holding her right arm).

In the more elaborate Jewish ceremonies the processional is led by the rabbi and the cantor.

After my father gives me away, I would like to give my mother a long-stemmed rose before the actual ceremony begins. How do I carry it up the aisle?

Carry it alongside your bouquet, as unobtrusively as possible so that when you present it to your mother it will be a surprise. You may also want to consider presenting one to your groom's mother as well.

We would like to write our own vows; how do we go about it?

Well, first of all, don't assume that you can do so; if you're having a religious ceremony, you will need to check with the officiant first to see if you are allowed to deviate from the traditional vows. If you are and you would like to create your own personal wedding vows, I recommend my book *Complete Book of Wedding Vows*, which will give you specific phrasing to work with, including vows for second marriages and vows with ethnic and religious variations. I don't have any statistics to prove it, but my feeling is that most of the brides and grooms today write their own vows, or at least change some of the wording to reflect their individual feelings of commitment to each other. I highly recommend writing your own vows if you are allowed to do so.

You've been to so many weddings. What is the number one goof that happens during the ceremony?

Probably the number one goof has to do with the aisle runner. You see, everyone seems to think that there's nothing to unrolling an aisle runner, but often when the ushers begin to unroll it just before the processional, it comes loose where it is attached at the front of the church or it rolls out crooked or wrinkled. I suggest that the ushers practice unrolling the aisle runner during the rehearsal or, better yet, do away with it altogether.

My fiance would like to walk his mother down the aisle, instead of having one of his ushers do it. Will this work out?

Of course. In fact, it is common for the groom to do this; then, he walks back down the aisle and hurries out a side door in time to join the officiant and his groomsmen in a side room before the ceremony begins.

We would like to stand facing the congregation during the ceremony, which means that our minister would have to have his back to the guests. Does this work out all right?

Yes, it works out just fine; in fact, it seems the most natural thing to do. That way everyone can see you as you recite your vows, etc.

What is the tradition of the "unity candle" and how can we incorporate it into our ceremony?

There are several versions of the unity candle ceremony, all with equal meaning. The idea is to have three candles: one small candle representing the bride's family, one small candle representing the groom's family and one larger, taller candle representing the unification of the two families. The two smaller candles may stand on each side of the altar with the larger candle on a taller stand in the center, or all three candles may be on one candle stand. The two smaller candles are usually lit at the beginning of the service, either by the candlelighters or by the mothers or parents of the bride and groom. They then burn throughout the service until the couple is pronounced husband and wife at which time they each walk to their respective family's candle, carry it to the unity candle where they light the larger unity candle at the same time. Then they blow out the smaller candles, leaving only the large unity candle burning as they return to their places at the front of the altar. This is usually a very touching, sometimes tearful, ceremony as two families and two hearts become one.

Chapter 15

The Reception

What's involved in planning a reception?

A wedding reception is probably the biggest party you and your family will ever plan, and there is a lot involved. Here is a list of the basics:

- The rental of the site itself.
- The theme for the decorations.
- Selection of a host or hostess.
- Hiring of a professional staff or recruitment of volunteers.
- The food menu.
- The beverage menu.
- Entertainment and presentations, including the musical selections to be performed or played.
- The rental or purchase of equipment.
- The signing of the guest book.
- The order of the receiving line, if you choose to have one.
- The dance order.
- The toasts.
- The wedding cake.
- Seating charts for the bride's table and parents' table.
- Favors, if you choose to have them.
- The bouquet throw and garter toss.

- The order of the reception.
- Arrangements for cleanup of the site.

Do you have any ideas for reception sites?

The most common sites are private clubs or halls, your church's social hall or garden, a restaurant or a hotel ball room. Surprisingly, some of the loveliest wedding reception sites belong to your state, county or city; make a few phone calls and see what they have available. The rental fees will run from quite reasonable ($500 for four hours), to several thousand dollars, depending on the site and whether you are a resident of that city or county. You'll find that the best public sites are reserved a year or more in advance, so time is of the essence.

As soon as you become engaged, you may want to hold off on setting your wedding date until you determine when your favorite ceremony and reception sites are available. Don't set a date first and then force everything else to fit around it. By the way, if you happen to know of a lovely site for your ceremony and/or reception, but it doesn't have a structure large enough to hold your guests, consider renting a large tent. I know of a couple who were offered the use of her aunt's and uncle's small beach house; they rented a large tent that extended from the deck out toward the water which is where the ceremony and reception took place. For another wedding, a tent was erected on the groom's grandparents' farm, right alongside the horses and cows. Tents are portable, remember, and can be erected almost anywhere.

What kind of reception is easiest to plan?

Hands down, the easiest and most hassle-free is a reception held in a hotel or private club that has full catering services, where everything is included in one price.

What percentage of the total cost of the wedding is usually spent on the reception?

The reception is the most expensive cost of all, ranging from 30 to 50 percent of your total expenditures. The two biggest expenses are the food and the band. You can beat the odds, obviously, by having a do-it-yourself "family potluck" buffet table and using amateur musical talent.

Is it absolutely necessary to have a receiving line? I always hate having to wait through them when I attend a wedding reception. Isn't there a better way?

A receiving line is usually in order for a very formal wedding; otherwise, there are several more relaxed alternatives. One very nice custom is to have the bride and groom, as well as the other members of the wedding party, "float" around the reception, speaking to each cluster of guests. Another custom, rather new but quite enjoyable and comfortable for the guests, is to have the guests remain seated in the church or synagogue until they are personally greeted and dismissed by the bride and groom themselves. This could be called the "lazy man's receiving line" because the guests remain seated until it's time for their row to stand and file past the bride and groom, hugging, kissing and wishing them well as they exit their pews.

What is the proper order for a receiving line?

First in line is the bride's mother, then the groom's mother, followed, of course, by the bride and groom. Next is the bride's honored attendant, followed by the bridesmaids. The presence of the fathers in the receiving line is optional, but if one father chooses to stand in the line, the other should do so as well. If they do choose to stand in the receiving line, this would be the order: bride's mother, groom's father, groom's mother, bride's father, bride, groom, bride's honored attendant and then the bridesmaids.

How much time should we allow for the receiving line?

Allow 30 to 40 minutes for every 200 guests.

Is there some rule about how elaborate the refreshments have to be for a formal wedding?

There used to be, but I've noticed that these rules have been relaxed and the formality of the reception doesn't necessarily follow the formality of the ceremony. For example, a formal wedding may be followed by very simple refreshments, such as champagne and wedding cake; on the other hand, a very simple ceremony may be followed by an elaborate sit-down dinner. One thing I've found, however, is that there are differences in customs around the country: Wedding breakfasts or sit-down dinners are common in New England; a cocktail party with finger foods in the late afternoon or early evening is a California thing; and dessert buffets are most popular in the south.

Are there rules of etiquette on what time of day each type of reception food is to be served?

Yes, but don't take them too seriously. Here they are:

Breakfast reception	9 a.m. to 11 a.m.
Brunch reception	11 a.m. to 1 p.m.
Luncheon reception	Noon to 2 p.m.
Tea reception	2 p.m. to 5 p.m.
Cocktail reception	4 p.m. to 7:30 p.m.
Dinner reception	7 p.m. to 9 p.m.

Are we expected to pay for meals for the musicians, photographer and videographer?

Yes, you should provide them with something to eat, although nothing as elaborate or expensive as the food you are serving your guests. Usually these contracted workers are provided with a simple hot plate or tray of sandwiches and chips. Work this out with your caterer ahead of time so that there are no misunderstandings.

What are "wedding day diaries"?

They are blank books or single sheets of paper that can later be made into a book that are placed at each reception table for the guests to write in, "waxing eloquent" with their thoughts about the day, their remembrances of their friendships with the bride or groom and their good wishes for the newlywed couple. The thoughts may be tender and poignant or clever and comedic, but in any case these little books or sheets of paper are gathered up and saved for the couple to read when they get back from their honeymoon.

Aren't there certain circumstances that justify a cash bar at a wedding reception?

No.

Are there certain traditions that must be followed during a wedding reception?

Only the toast to the couple and a wedding cake; everything else is optional.

Are we expected to serve wedding cake at a breakfast reception? Won't that seem strange to serve dessert at 9 a.m.?

No, not if the cake is a light one filled and topped with fruits, such as berries, and served with sherbet or whipped cream topping.

I have six aunts who have generously offered to bake and cook all the food for the reception as their wedding gift to us. Although we really appreciate this, we do want the buffet table and the service to appear to be professional. What can we do?

Congratulations on having such generous relatives! Did you know that the reception food is usually the biggest expense of the entire wedding? Now, the trick is to give it a "pricey presentation," so you'll want all this lovely food to be presented in an elegant way—after all, this isn't just another church potluck, is it? You'll need a long table, or two tables placed end to end that can be "skirted" (with disposable ruffled paper skirting) and covered with the most expensive-looking white damask linen or lace table-cloths you can find. You'll also need a dramatic centerpiece, such as an ice sculpture (do it yourself with an inexpensive mold purchased from your catering supply store), or a large flower arrangement (borrow one from the ceremony); then, you'll need to cascade the food dishes from the back to the front of the table by elevating them. Stacks of oversized books work well, as do heavy pots turned upside down or even cigar boxes filled with bricks. Just be sure they are all covered with white linen cloths or napkins, creating a white staircase effect, then fill the spaces in between with flowers, ribbons, fresh fruit or bottles of champagne, beau-tifully wrapped about their necks with white silk flowers and ribbons. Then place the food dishes on these elevated mounds, mirroring them on the table so that there is one of each dish at each end of the table. By the way, garnish the trays of food as well, adding huge whole strawberries, melon slices, large wedges of fresh pineapple or fresh flowers.

What is a "marriage cup"?

This is a cup placed at the bride's table that is used, ac-cording to old-world tradition, by the bride and groom prior to their first toast. There are two types of marriage cup. The first is called the *Nuremberg Cup,* which is usually sil-ver, made in the shape of a young girl with a large skirt, holding a cup over her head. The bride and groom drink from this cup at the same time. The second type of mar-riage cup is *French,* made in the shape of a small bowl on a pedestal. The bride drinks from this cup first, followed, of course, by her groom. Whichever cup is used, tradition says, as the bride and groom drink from it, they plight their troth.

Is it a good idea to have someone on hand to supervise the reception?

Yes. You can have someone serve in an official capacity as a host, hostess or master of ceremonies, or you may just have someone (a close friend or relative) who has volunteered to see to it that everything runs smoothly, from the receiving line, to the food service, to the cake cutting, to the first dance, etc. Be sure to give this dear person a *wonderful* thank-you gift for performing this monumental task.

What's a "food station"?

A food station is the latest fad for serving reception food. Each station is a separate table that serves a certain type of food. For example, you may have a seafood table, a prime rib table (where a chef stands carving), an hors d'oeuvres table, a fruit and cheese table, etc. Of course, you will also have a special station for your wedding cake. The nice thing about food stations is that many guests can be served at once because these tables are spread all over the reception hall. In the case of economical reception foods, such as finger sandwiches, chips and dip or crackers and cheese, food stations can make simple foods seem like "more." The guests enjoy the concept, too, because it gives them a chance to move around the room, visiting with other guests clustered around the various stations.

Is it possible for a catering service to prepare recipes provided to them by our family? We have certain traditional ethnic foods that are usually served at our family weddings, but we don't want to go through the work of preparing them ourselves.

Yes, it is not at all unusual for a caterer to be asked to prepare a family favorite. As a matter of fact, if truth be known, caterers get tired of fixing the same old things week after week and they enjoy the challenge!

Do you have any clever ideas for favors that don't cost a fortune?

I've seen some really fun and original favors lately; here are some of them:

- Decorate the handle of a 10-inch candle with tufted netting, tiny silk flowers and narrow dangling ribbons; at the end of the reception give one to each guest to light and use to form a "going-away" path for the bride and groom. This only works, of course, for an evening wedding.

- Give each guest a decorated packet of seeds with a personalized note attached that reads something like this: "As these seeds bloom into flowers, may they remind you of how much we love you."

- Use this same idea, only with a tiny tree sapling. (They are available at very little cost from your state forestry department).

- Give each guest a bottle of bubble blowing liquid, wrapped in lace or tulle netting and tied at the neck with a narrow ribbon. Then, during your first dance, the guests can blow bubbles over you (a la Lawrence Welk) and as you leave the reception they can create a shower of bubbles as you rush to your getaway car.

- As each single guest or couple arrives at the reception, have their photo taken using a Polaroid camera; then, attach each photo to a designated tree at the reception, along with a loving note from the bride and groom thanking the guest for sharing the day, etc. The photos are then given as favors to the guests as they leave the reception.

- If it's a Christmas wedding, give each guest a special ornament customized with the names of the bride and groom and the wedding date. This idea works well with wooden rocking horses, plain glass ball ornaments and most bread dough ornaments, such as a wreath, stocking or gingerbread house.

- For a Polynesian theme, give each guest a fresh or silk flower lei or inexpensive shell lei which can be purchased at an oriental import outlet.
- Write a personalized message in black calligraphy onto a piece of parchment which then can be rolled and tied with a narrow satin ribbon in your wedding colors. Make up a master and have it copied onto 8½ x 14 sheets of parchment paper; each sheet will provide nine scrolls.
- Order chocolate kisses from The Hershey Company (800-233-2168) wrapped in silver foil or various pastel colored foils. Sprinkle them generously along the center of all the tables.
- Create your own customized bookmarks on your word processor that include your names, wedding date, your vows and a thank-you message.

We know the bride and groom have the first dance, but what is the dance order after that?

After the bride and groom have danced together, here is the normal order:

- The bride's father cuts in on the groom to dance with his daughter while the groom dances with his new mother-in-law.
- The bride dances with the groom's father while the groom dances with his own mother.
- The bride dances with the best man while the groom dances with the honored bridal attendant.
- The DJ or band leader then invites the rest of the guests to join in.
- Sometime during the reception, be sure the bride dances with each groomsman and the groom with each bridal attendant.

When you think about it, this is all pretty logical, but don't get flustered if the order doesn't go exactly as planned. No one will notice or care.

My parents were divorced and remarried, as were my fiance's. How do we handle the dance sequence at the reception without hurting feelings?

My suggestion is to forego the normal sequence and emphasize you and your groom's first dance together, followed by everyone joining in, beginning with the bridal attendants and their dance partners. Later on, after the parents have danced with their spouses, it would be appropriate for you and your fiance to exchange partners with them.

I've heard some real horror stories about caterers who add on so many unexpected charges. What can we do to protect ourselves?

Again, as I always say, no matter whose services you are engaging, *always* get it in writing. If the caterer's contract doesn't include everything that was represented to you, write it in and have the caterer initial it. Here are some things to have clearly understood in advance:

- If you're purchasing a certain "wedding package" from the caterer, *exactly* what does it include?
- What does a sample place setting consist of?
- What decorations, if any, are included in the price?
- Will all tables be "skirted" at their expense? (A paper skirt that wraps the table from the tabletop to the floor.)
- Exactly how much food and drink will be provided per guest?
- What about an open bar? Exactly what are the charges? And what are the brands that will be served?
- What is the policy on champagne? Are there pouring fees? Cake cutting fees? Cleanup fees? Bartender fees? Hostess fees?

- Will you be required to purchase your wedding cake from them? Or may you furnish your own from another source?
- How many servers will be provided for their fee?
- Will they set up all the tables in advance?
- Are they covered by insurance against china or crystal breakage? If not, are you allowed to purchase insurance?
- Exactly how much do they charge to extend the reception past the agreed hour?
- When is the deadline for your guest count?
- Are taxes and gratuities included in the contract?

What is a "groom's cake"?

Traditionally, this is the cake, a piece of which a maiden placed under her pillow the night after a wedding so that she may dream of the man she is to marry; however, you don't find a groom's cake at many weddings these days, but when you do it is usually a dark cake, either chocolate or fruitcake. Often the cake is baked in advance, cut into small squares and packaged into white or gold boxes for the guests to take home with them as a momento of the wedding. In some cultures it is common for several relatives to go together to provide this cake as a wedding gift, baking and wrapping it in advance. Instead of using boxes, the cake may be wrapped in shiny white paper and tied with ribbons. A groom's cake may also be cut and served during the reception, a tasty choice for those who prefer chocolate or fruitcake over the traditional white bride's cake.

When is the wedding cake usually cut?

The cutting of the bride's cake should be a ceremony in itself, with lights, music and great fanfare. If a sit-down meal is served, the cake is usually cut right after the meal so it can be served as dessert. However, if the menu is lighter, such as a brunch, luncheon or finger food buffet, the cake-cutting ceremony is usually the last "hurrah" before the bride tosses the bouquet, the groom tosses the garter and they leave the reception. (Often, however, the bride and groom do stay awhile following these events.)

What is a "Fairmont cake presentation"?

This is an especially dramatic presentation where the cake is kept hidden until the very last minute. Finally, the lights are lowered and the music fades and everyone quiets in anticipation of the presentation. Then, as the cake is wheeled out into the middle of the room, it is spotlighted as the music plays "Here Comes the Bride." At this point, everyone gathers around the cake and proceeds to "ooh" and "aah" as the bride and groom cut the cake.

What is a "ribbon pull"?

Before the bride and groom cut the cake, the bridesmaids gather around the wedding cake and each pull a ribbon (attached to a silver or gold charm) from between the frosted layers. Usually, each charm is different, from a heart to a horseshoe to a four leaf clover, but the bridesmaid who pulls out the ring charm is considered the luckiest of all because it is said she will be the next to marry.

My aunt insists we open our wedding gifts during the reception. She says it's not fair to the guests if we don't. I've never seen gifts opened at any reception I've attended. Why is that?

Because, although your aunt may not understand the reasoning, it is actually *unfair* to the guests to take their time opening your gifts. The gifts should be assembled in a safe place to be opened after your honeymoon; meanwhile, enjoy the reception and be sure to visit with the guests.

What about having a gift display at the reception? This sounds like a lot of trouble to me.

First of all, this is usually only done at a home wedding, never in a hotel or club, so it shouldn't be that much trouble. It is just a matter of designating a room or corner where gifts that have been previously opened may be displayed, with or without their cards. The guests enjoy seeing the gifts and it might even be fun for you and your groom to look them over during the festivities. By the way, any checks should be displayed in such a way that they overlap, showing the name at the bottom of the check, but not the amount. Cover the top check with an attractive paper weight that will do double-duty, covering the amount on the top check as well as holding all the checks in place so they don't scoot around on the table.

Although we don't normally drink champagne, we do plan to serve it at our reception. What kind of champagne is best, and how many bottles do we need for 200 guests?

Champagne varies as to dryness: "Brut" is very dry (usually served with a meal); "Extra Dry" is not as dry as "Brut" (usually served with desserts or after meals); and "Dry" or "sec" is the least dry and the most popular for sipping. The latter is probably the most popular champagne served at wedding receptions because everyone seems to like it. As far as quantity is concerned, it depends on whether it will be served only for the toast, which would require one glass per adult guest, or for sipping throughout the reception, which would require two glasses per person. A bottle of champagne has about 25 ounces which will fill six generous glasses or eight small glasses. At one small glass per guest, you would need 200 servings or 25 bottles. By the way, to cut down on costs you may want to serve a less expensive sparkling wine instead, such as a sparkling spumante, rose, chablis or cold duck. Another way to economize is to serve a champagne punch instead where one bottle can stretch to serve about 13 guests.

You mention serving champagne for the toast; who makes the first toast to the bride and groom?

The best man always makes the first toast, using a microphone if necessary, followed by the two fathers, the groom to his bride, the bride to her groom (if she feels comfortable doing so) and then, finally, toasts may be made by other members of the bridal party, as well as any of the guests who may wish to do so.

What does someone usually say when he toasts the bride and groom?

The ideal toast is short and sweet; here is a typical toast to the couple: "To Bill and Janie and a lifetime of good health, happiness and prosperity."

What is the difference between "French service" and "plate service"?

A big one! *French service* is more formal: When the guests are seated at their tables they will find that their plates already contain fruit cups and other appetizers; then servers wheel carts to each table to serve the rest of the meal tableside, placing each food item onto the guests' plates individually. *Plate service*, however, simply means that the plates are prepared in the kitchen, brought out and served. Obviously, plate service is much less expensive.

Our wedding is planned for one in the afternoon with the reception immediately following at the same location. We need to leave no later than 5 p.m., so this will allow about three hours for the reception. Can you give me a suggested timetable for the reception itself?

Assuming your formal photographs will be taken before the wedding and that you, having an afternoon wedding, will only be serving a light buffet of some kind, here is a possible timetable:

2 p.m.	The bridal party stands in the receiving line as the musicians play background music.
2:45 p.m.	The bridal party is seated at the bride's table where they will be served; the designated host or hostess invites the guests to line up for the buffet.
3:30 p.m.	The musicians begin to play livelier dance music and the bride and groom begin their "first dance," followed by other traditional pairings (the groom with his mother, etc.) and finally by the rest of the guests.
4 p.m.	The musicians stop playing as the best man offers the first toast, followed by toasts from the groom to his bride, his parents and his new in-laws. The bride may also offer toasts to her groom, his parents and her parents at this time, but only if she feels comfortable doing so.
4:15 p.m.	After the toasts, the best man or host invites the guests to gather around the cake table for the cake-cutting ceremony. The cake is then served to the guests.
4:30 p.m.	Time for the bride's bouquet toss and the groom's garter toss.
4:45 p.m.	The bride and groom slip away to change into their going-away outfits and say private goodbyes to their parents while the musicians continue to play and, hopefully, the guests continue to dance, visit and enjoy themselves.

5 p.m.　　　The bride and groom then dash through a spray of rice, birdseed or rose petals that are showered over them by the wedding guests as the couple jumps into their getaway vehicle and zooms off to their fabulous honeymoon.

As you can see, a three-hour reception goes by very quickly and, unless you have a responsible person charged with orchestrating the events, the time can get away from you. So, if it's crucial that you leave the reception by 5 p.m., you must appoint someone to monitor the timetable. After you're off, by the way, your parents have the choice of extending the dancing and partying as long as they wish, or ending the festivities by subtly discontinuing the music and thanking the guests for coming.

I would like to save my bouquet and have it preserved somehow after the wedding, so what can I throw at the bouquet toss?

Do what most brides do these days: have a "pretend" bouquet made up ahead of time, out of fresh or silk flowers. If you have an arm bouquet of long-stemmed flowers, you may toss one or two of them, saving the rest as a momento of your wedding.

Can you give me some theme ideas for our reception?

You can carry your ceremony theme through to your reception, if you would like, or you can use one of these ideas:

- Spring garden party.
- Country-western.
- Nostalgia.
- Polynesian.
- 50s sock hop.
- Gay 90s.
- Mississippi riverboat.

- Mountain ski resort.
- Winter wonderland.
- Renaissance festival.
- Roaring 20s.
- Christmas.
- Paris in springtime.
- Cupids and hearts.
- Victorian tea party.
- Romantic candlelight.
- The Love Boat.
- Ethnic themes (Mexican fiesta, Scandinavian love feast, African safari, German Oktoberfest).
- A theme customized especially for the couple, such as an airport theme if either the groom or the bride is a pilot, or a race car theme for the groom who's into stock car racing, etc.

The main thing to remember is that you don't want your reception, or your ceremony for that matter, to have that same old cookie-cutter look. You want your wedding to be the one the guests are still talking about a year later. Try for originality!

We would like to have a smoke-free reception; how can we let our guests know this in a tactful way?

You can place "Thank You for Not Smoking" cards on each table or around the reception hall, but instead of banning smoking altogether, you may want to designate an outdoor smoking area, in which case you can post a sign near the guest book saying, "A smoking area has been provided on the east patio." By the way, be sure to have the catering staff remove all ashtrays from the premises.

What's a "dummy wedding cake"?

This is a fake cake made out of Styrofoam layers, like the display cakes in bakery windows. Dummy cakes have become popular because they allow you to have a larger, more elegant cake for a fraction of the cost of a "real" one, without sacrificing the quality of the cake served to the guests. Purchase the inexpensive Styrofoam layers at a hobby or bakery supply store and build a cake as high and wide as you would like; you can even have side cakes with "bridges" connecting them to the center cake. The top layer should be the real thing, however, so it can be removed and frozen, to be served on the couple's first wedding anniversary. Frost the entire cake with a simple white butter frosting and then decorate the layers with fresh or silk flowers, trailing ivy or ribbons. You can even add lights and a bubbling fountain, if you'd like. When the bride and groom cut the cake to serve each other bites, they cut from a small cake that sits between them and the wedding cake, or a wedge of real cake may be inserted ahead of time into the bottom layer of Styrofoam, frosted over in such a way that only the bride and groom know it's there. Then, after the cake-cutting ceremony, the guests are quickly served slices of cake cut from frosted white sheet cakes that have been stashed in the kitchen. Amazingly, the guests never catch on to this whole thing!

Do you have any original ideas for cake toppers? Everything I've seen has been the same old thing—and for no small price!

If you want something different and affordable, here are a few ideas:

- Purchase fresh flowers from your supermarket or wholesale florist. Have someone arrange them on top of the cake as soon as it is delivered to the reception by the bakery. The flowers can also be trailed down from layer to layer. Be sure you don't underestimate the beauty of decorating your cake with fresh flowers—even Whitney Houston's wedding cake was decorated simply with fresh violets.

- Use a wine glass filled with roses and baby's breath. Set the wine glass on top of a round mirror and fill it with flowers and narrow ribbons that spill over onto the mirror. You can also arrange a ring of flowers around the perimeter of the mirror, where the edge of the mirror touches the frosting.
- Try a tiny white basket filled with the same, sitting on a round mirror or directly on the frosting itself.
- Place a blown glass figurine set on a mirror, with small rose buds and baby's breath around the base of the figurine.
- Use a Precious Moments bride and groom. There are several available. Does anyone in your family collect these figurines? Ask around.
- Try a teddy bear bride and groom. Dress up a pair of tiny teddy bears with a little white veil for the bride and bow tie or tuxedo jacket for the groom.
- Decide on a customized topper. Depending on your theme or your hobbies, you may be able to come up with something truly original. If you're really into downhill skiing, for example, you can make tiny skis out of tongue depressors; paint your names on the skis, tie them with white satin ribbons and "plunge" them into the"snow" of the frosting. Put on your thinking caps and come up with an idea all your own.

Other than the dummy wedding cake idea, what are some other ways we can cut down on the cost of the cake?

The average cost of a wedding cake these days is about $450, so it's no wonder brides are looking for some ways to cut down. One of the best ways, which I've done myself several times lately, is to order the cake from your super-market bakery. In our little California valley town, the bakery at Albertson's Supermarket happens to have the best cakes for the money—they are not only moist and delicious, but decorated as professionally as any you will find. The key is to watch for their sales and order the cake ahead of time during the sale, even though the wedding date may be some months off. Then, on the day before the wedding, you'll need to have someone pick it up, and it comes disassembled, by the way. But don't let this throw you because it's easy to put together. Each layer has a plastic plate at its base with ready-made "innies" for the columns' "outies." The innies and outies fit together nice and tight as you assemble the cake at the site. You don't have to worry about transporting a fully-assembled cake, four or five layers high, balanced on spindly columns, in a van or something, like you see in the movies. Another suggestion is to have the cake made by someone who does this out of her home; ask to see photos of other cakes she has done, along with recommendations of other brides who have used her. My last suggestion is only logical: Order a smaller wedding cake, but supplement with homemade sheet cakes.

By the way, don't be disappointed if you don't remember what the cake tasted like; you'll have your chance to really enjoy it when you drag the top layer out of your freezer on your first wedding anniversary. Most brides and grooms are so excited by the time the cake is cut they hardly remember the event at all, much less what the cake tasted like. The only bride I ever heard of who actually enjoyed her wedding cake was Roseanne when she married her ex-bodyguard, Ben Thomas. Guests at her wedding said she went back for thirds!

What's the worst cake disaster you've ever seen?

The very worst was when the top two layers of the wedding cake slid onto the floor. It was a hot July day and the fresh whipped cream filling (the only thing holding the layers together) melted. This was pretty disastrous because they had to make do with the one remaining layer. Another case was more humorous than disastrous: The family dog jumped up on a chair and helped himself to half a layer while everyone was out of the room. Moral of the story: Use butter cream icing and send Fido on a mini-vacation to his favorite kennel until after the wedding.

What is a "menu board"?

It is simply a board that tells what is on the menu for your reception dinner or buffet. All the items on the menu are elegantly listed in calligraphy on a piece of parchment which is matted, framed and placed on a floor or table easel.

We're in a quandary about whether to serve alcohol at our reception. We've heard that the bride and groom can be held liable for a drunken guest who then causes an accident or something. Is this true?

Yes, in most states it is, which is why more and more couples are either doing away with alcohol altogether or serving it only in the form of a mild champagne punch. At the very least, the drinks should be limited so that, for example, there are a maximum of two glasses of champagne allowed per guest. If you have an *open bar* or a *cash bar* you are asking for trouble, not only from a liability standpoint, but from the standpoint of risking the beauty and joy of your reception by having a guest or two become unruly, obscene or obnoxious—you certainly don't need that!

Other than the ideas you've already mentioned, do you have any other suggestions for cutting down on the cost of the reception?

Yes. Here are a few:

- Purchase sparkling wine by the box at a ridiculously low price (check out your discount grocery stores and food warehouses, such as Costco or Sam's Club). Then, pour the wine into carafes, one for each table.
- Rather than rent crystal or china, borrow it or use paper products instead.

- Call local vocational schools who offer programs in food service or decoration; hire their students or recent graduates.
- Cut down on the size of your guest list.
- Have two receptions—a simple cake and punch reception for all your guests served immediately following the ceremony, followed by a more elaborate reception later in the day for close friends and family.
- If you only have a few relatives who offer to bring food dishes to the reception—not enough food to fill the buffet table—supplement the donations with side dishes ordered from your neighborhood grocery store delicatessen.

Do we need some kind of security when it comes to guarding our wedding gifts?

It's a shame to say, but yes. You see, not only can gifts "grow legs" and disappear, but cards even more so. Be especially careful of any cards that contain checks or money. If you have a basket on display at your gift table to collect your cards, be sure it is emptied frequently throughout the reception. If your reception is being held at a club, restaurant or hotel, there may already be a security officer available to keep an eye on your gifts as well as any "overly happy" guests who may be getting a little out of hand. This security officer, whether provided by you or the facility itself, should also be in charge of designating drivers for any guests who may have had just one too many glasses of champagne!

Is it necessary to include the garter toss and bouquet throw during our reception?

Actually, more and more couples, particularly those who are older and consider themselves a little more sophisticated, are eliminating both of these traditional ceremonies.

What about shooting off fireworks at the reception?

This is becoming quite a fad, and it doesn't have to be a fourth of July wedding either. Usually the fireworks display takes place after dark as the bride and groom take off in their getaway vehicle.

What happens after the reception? What things need to be done?

Unfortunately, there are still a number of details to be tended to. Here they are:

- The ceremony and reception sites need to be "undecorated" and cleaned. Hopefully, your families will receive help with these chores!
- All the "precious" things need to be gathered up and transported to the bride's family's home, such as the top layer of the wedding cake, the cake top itself, the guest books, floral arrangements, wedding gifts and the inevitable leftover wedding favors, ceremony programs, unity candle, etc.
- Retrieve the bride's and groom's wedding attire, if they changed into their going-away clothes at the reception site. Take special care with the wedding gown, which should be taken to a dry cleaner for preservation as soon as feasible.
- All rental equipment and clothing must be returned. The best man should see that all the men's rental attire is returned.
- Pay all hired staff with cash or check, including the musicians and caterer.
- Decide what to do about leftover food and drink; there may be unopened bottles of champagne or wine that were included in the prepaid catering fee.
- Thank all hired and volunteer staff, including the host or hostess, if applicable.

- Search the ceremony and reception sites for any belongings your guests may have accidentally left behind, such as gloves, umbrella, coat or jacket.
- Provide transportation for any guests who got carried away with "toasts" and need a designated driver.

With all the hundreds of weddings I've been involved in, the biggest reception mistake I've seen is a lack of planning for the "after-wedding cleanup." My suggestion is to plan ahead by recruiting designated helpers to lighten this load.

Chapter 16

Photography and Videography

How soon should we start shopping for a photographer?

The sooner, the better—even before you've set the wedding date. Shopping for an excellent photographer who is also affordable is a great treasure hunt. To begin the hunt, ask other brides who they used, what they were charged and how they liked the photographs. Then, get on the telephone and begin calling some of these photographers. Most will ask you to come in for a consultation at which time you will see samples of his or her work and receive price lists for various wedding packages. After you've visited several of these artists, you'll have a feel for which style suits you best. Some photographers are demanding perfectionists and are known for their flawless formal poses; others excel in their creative, candid shots; and some are easier to work with than others. If you've found a photographer you think might work for you, have him take your engagement photo to see how you like him first before hiring him to photograph your entire wedding.

I don't want my fiance to see my wedding gown until I come down the aisle. I've been told that photographers hate this. Why?

Because it means they have to rush to take all the photographs after the ceremony, while your guests are waiting for you at the reception. Many couples are disregarding this tradition and posing for all their formal shots an hour and a half to two hours before the ceremony. However, if you are really determined to "wow" your groom as you come down the aisle, then hold fast and don't let anyone talk you out of it. One solution is for the photographer to take as many photographs as possible before the ceremony that *don't* involve the bride and groom together. For example, all the photographs that include you—either alone, or with your parents or with your bridesmaids and other attendants. Of course, the photographer can do the same with your fiance and his family, groomsmen, etc.

Does the photographer take pictures during the ceremony?

He or she shouldn't; nothing is more distracting than the flashing and clicking of the camera during the ceremony itself. However, he or she will probably take photographs at the rear of the church as each member of the wedding party enters and leaves the site. (A photographer with the right equipment, however, can take photographs during the ceremony, zooming in on a timed shot from quite a distance away, with no flash required, or mounting the camera out of the congregation's view, on a balcony, for example.)

My parents are divorced, but on good terms with each other. Is it proper to have them stand beside me in a photograph?

Usually divorced parents do not appear together in the same photograph, but you may certainly use your own judgment on this—it's your wedding. What most brides do is have separate photographs taken, one with each parent.

What are some questions we should ask before signing a contract with a photographer?

In addition to the answers to these questions, be sure everything else you discuss and agree upon is put *in writing* so there are no misunderstandings:

- What does the wedding package include? How many albums? How many photos? What sizes? How many proofs? How many formal shots? How many candid shots?
- Is the bride's formal portrait included?
- How many proofs will we have to select from?
- How many hours will the photographer be on duty? Will he or she stay until the end of the reception for the cake-cutting ceremony?
- If we decide to order extra copies of certain shots, how much will they cost?

What's the difference between a "studio photographer" and a "wedding photographer"?

A *studio photographer* takes photographs in his studio where the settings and lighting are controlled; a *wedding photographer* specializes in taking formal and candid photographs on location at various sites, such as the bride's home, the church and the reception site where very little is controlled, from the subjects to the settings to the lighting.

Will the photographer take a few shots of us at other sites?

Yes, if you arrange with him ahead of time. Many couples like to scout out interesting spots for additional photos, such as a nearby garden or park or, perhaps, someplace very special to them. Do your homework now before things get too busy and take a walk around your ceremony and reception sites looking for unique backdrops for a few extra photographs; your photographer will appreciate your effort and will be glad to incorporate your suggestions.

Can we give the photographer a list of the photographs we want him to take?

Yes. In fact, he will appreciate having your list of "must" shots; most of them will probably be on his list already, but there will be others that are unique to your own individual wedding and he has no way to know what they are unless you tell him. I suggest you make up a master list of all the photos you want for your album. Be sure to give him this list ahead of time so there will be no surprises. Here are some poses you may want to include on your list; I have separated them into formal and candid shots:

Formal:
- The bride alone.
- The bride and groom.
- The bride with her parents.
- The groom with his parents.
- The bride with her mother.
- The bride with her father.
- The groom with his mother.
- The groom with his father.
- The bride with her attendants.
- The bride with her honored attendant.
- The groom with his groomsmen and ushers.
- The bride with the groomsmen.
- The groom with his best man.
- The groom with the bridal attendants.
- The bride with the children in the wedding party.
- The groom with the children in the wedding party.
- The bride and groom with the entire wedding party.
- The bride and groom with the bride's family.
- The bride and groom with the groom's family.
- The bride with her grandparents.
- The groom with his grandparents.
- The bride and her father walking up the aisle.

- The bride and groom kneeling in prayer.
- The bride and groom lighting the unity candle.
- The bride and groom exchanging vows.
- The bride and groom kissing.
- The bride and groom walking down the aisle.
- The bride and groom cutting the cake.
- The bride and groom feeding each other the cake.
- The bride and groom toasting each other.
- A close-up of the couple's hands, showing their wedding rings.
- The bride's mother as she is being ushered down the aisle.

Candids:

- The bride's mother or maid of honor helping with her veil.
- The bride dressing at home or at the ceremony site.
- The bride's father with the bride at home or arriving at the ceremony site.
- An outdoor shot with a sunrise or sunset in the distance.
- If it's snowing, a shot "hanging out" with a snowman (built ahead of time by the bridesmaids and groomsmen and dressed in a top hat or a scarf in the wedding colors).
- If the wedding is held on a ranch or out in the country, a shot of the couple sitting on a fence or with their arms around the necks of a couple horses, etc.
- A shot of the bride's and groom's empty wedding shoes, sitting side by side.
- A shot of the bride or groom with his or her arms around a family pet.

- If it's raining, a shot of the couple "Singing in the Rain" while dancing with an umbrella overhead.
- Special shots with certain friends or family members.
- The bride and groom as they are "announced" upon their arrival at the reception.
- Shots of guests as they pass through the receiving line.
- Close-ups of the cake table, buffet table, centerpieces, special decorations.
- Random shots taken during the reception.
- The best man as he is toasting the bride and groom.
- The bride and groom's first dance.
- The bride and groom each dancing with others.
- The bride tossing her bouquet.
- The groom tossing the bride's garter.
- The bride and groom telling their parents goodbye before they leave the reception.
- The guests as they shower the couple with confetti, birdseed, etc.
- The bride and groom driving off in their getaway vehicle.

How can we be sure we are hiring a reputable, honest photographer?

There are a couple ways: Ask for references, preferably from people you know and trust, or look for photographers who are members of the Professional Photographers of America. You can write this organization (P.P.O.A., Membership Department, 1090 Executive Way, Des Plaines, IL 60018) for a brochure entitled "What Every Bride Should Know About Wedding Photography." Be sure to enclose a self-addressed stamped envelope.

Can our ceremony be videotaped?

Because a video camera is relatively quiet, this is usually not a problem unless it is against the church's policy.

What are questions I should ask the videographer?

First of all, ask the videographer if you can preview several tapes of weddings he has done. Don't choose a videographer until you have seen the quality of his work. Also, get everything in writing, just as with the photographer, and ask these questions:

- Will you be attending the rehearsal?
- What kind of video camera do you have? Do you have more than one, as a backup?
- How many fully-charged battery packs will you bring?
- What quality of tape will you be using?
- How many hours will you be in attendance during the ceremony and reception?
- How many hours of taped video will you provide?
- Do you conduct live interviews during the reception?
- How much do you charge for additional copies of the master tape?
- Do you furnish references?
- Do you furnish demo tapes we can view before making our decision?
- Does the video tape include voice-overs, captions, music and other special effects?

What are some of these "special effects" that videographers offer?

There are many, but here are a few:

- **Split screens.** Placing two different images on the screen at once.
- **Dissolving.** One image dissolves into the next, and so on.
- **Digital slides.** One image slides off one side of the screen and another slides on from the opposite side.
- **Skip-frame.** This allows a series of frames to skip at regular intervals, giving a sort of strobe effect.
- **Audio dubbing and mixing.** This allows you to replace the taped audio sound with something you've chosen, such as your favorite love song or a certain musical soundtrack.
- **Titling.** A title generator adds titles and subtitles during the editing phase after the actual filming.

What is a "disposable camera"?

It's a camera that is used once and then thrown away. It has become a trend to leave one of these cameras on each table for guests to snap candid shots during the reception. At the end of the day all these little cameras are gathered up and given to the couple to have developed when they get back from their honeymoon. These photos usually capture the true spirit of the celebration by catching special looks, humorous incidents and touching relationships missed by the professional photographer. I highly recommend these little cameras.

How can we be sure all these disposable cameras are left for us at the reception?

There have been some misunderstandings about these cameras from time to time; some guests thought they were favors or souvenirs and they took them home. Others took them home inadvertently or to use up any unused shots before having the film developed. To avoid any of these problems, attach a tactful note to each camera that explains the rules. You'll want the guests to know that the *purpose* of the cameras is for the bride and groom to have candid, spontaneous shots taken at random by anyone who would like to try his hand at photography. Then, to be sure all the cameras are gathered up near the end of the reception, designate several teenaged helpers to walk around the room with baskets to collect the cameras, *whether all the shots have been taken or not.*

It's scary to think of using an amateur photographer because what do we do if the pictures don't turn out? Do you think it's worth the risk?

I definitely think it's worth it because, with a few tricks, there won't be a risk. Here are those tricks:

- Be sure your amateur photographer uses a *quality* camera with a flash arm that is at least eight inches away from the lens (to prevent "red eye" photos). If your talented amateur only has a regular 35-millimeter camera, rent a good professional camera for him to use; it will only cost you about $75—well worth it!

- Ask all your other amateur friends to take photos as well, just for back-up. This includes the formals as well as the candids.

- Have your ceremony and reception videotaped which will give you added assurance since a video tape can be "freeze-framed" into still photos if necessary. This is an expensive procedure, but at least it is possible in case *all* of your amateur photographers muff their shots—but they won't.

- Finally, provide a supply of those disposable cameras described earlier in this chapter; encourage your guests to click away.

What is "red-eye"?

This is the spooky red glow in the eyes of those being photographed; it is caused by having the flash too close to the lens. This problem can be avoided by having a professional camera with the flash mounted at least eight inches away from the lens.

If we do decide to use an amateur photographer, do you have any tips for him so that the photos will look as professional as possible?

Yes. Here are a few suggestions for your talented friend:

- When taking outdoor shots, don't force the people to look into the sun which will cause them to squint. Also, keep the light exposure uniform so that everyone in the shot is either in the sun or in the shadow, not half and half.

- When posing the subjects for the shot, use some originality; don't line them up like a row of soldiers, for example, but cluster them in creative ways.

- Be aware of peculiar backgrounds. You don't want a branch "growing" out of someone's ear.

- Take a lot of candids and close-ups; capture the hugs and the tender moments.

- Use twice as much film as you planned, doubling your chances of success.

- Try to act as professional as possible by not becoming loud, stressed or hysterical; at least pretend you are calm and under control.

Any other ways we can save on the photography?

You might hire a professional photographer for the formal wedding pictures only, then use an amateur for the candids. Another idea is to check out colleges or trade schools for advanced photography students who may be interested in taking the shots, then turning over the film to you for processing when you get back from your honeymoon. Other cost-cutting ideas are hiring the photographer for an hourly fee, not as part of a package deal, and cutting down on the number of candid shots required by creating your own albums from the disposable camera shots or guests' own candids.

What about having an amateur videographer?

The trick here is to have *several* people taping the wedding and reception; all you need to do is provide the video tapes. Here are some tips for a professional result:

- Think "slow" for every shot. Not only move the camera slowly as you tape, but zoom in and out as slowly as possible, and leave the camera running on each shot much longer than you think necessary. This will keep the viewers from becoming seasick as they watch the tape after the wedding; there is nothing worse than a tape that jumps from shot to shot.

- Capture the tender moments: the looks, the hugs, the kisses, the tears. In fact, at the slightest hint of a tear, zoom in tight on the person's face and stay there until you're forced to move on.

- Use this ratio: 10 percent wide shots and 90 percent closeup.

- Tape as many live interviews as possible before and after the ceremony, as well as during the entire reception.

What does the term "soft focus" mean?

The photographer uses a special lens to create a filmy, romantic look to your photograph. You might want to have a few shots taken with this lens, but not too many or the novelty will wear off.

What are the average costs of a photographer and videographer?

The average cost of a wedding photographer is about $1,000, less in the Midwest and more in the metropolitan areas. The average cost of a wedding videographer is about $500, also less in the Midwest and more in the big cities.

Chapter 17

The Flowers

Can you give me an idea of what a florist charges for an average-priced wedding?

It depends on where you live. The metropolitan areas of California and the northeastern states are the highest, while the central mountain states are the lowest, the nationwide average being about $640. This price doesn't include flowers for the reception, however, or any extras, such as flowers for the wedding cake, extra corsages and boutonnieres or any special treatments, such as a decorated bird bath.

What percentage of the total wedding budget is spent on the flowers?

Usually 8 to 12 percent.

I'd like to talk to several florists before hiring one to do our wedding. Are florists offended by this?

If they are true professionals, they shouldn't be. You should feel free to walk into any florist in town and ask to see photographs of floral arrangements and bouquets they have created for other weddings they have done; and they should be willing to offer several written wedding plans that vary in total cost and what they include. Every florist will give you something new and interesting to consider, as well, especially if they have decorated ceremony or reception sites for other weddings. By the time you make your decision, you should feel very confident about your choice. One word of advice: Don't ever trust a florist who says, "Don't worry about anything, just leave it all up to me."

What are some ways we can cut down on the total cost of the flowers?

You can use fresh flowers and greenery from your own gardens or those of your friends and family; you can use existing decorations, shared from a previous wedding, or already in place because of the season; you can use silk flowers to make up all the corsages, boutonnieres and bouquets in advance, plus silk ficus and other flowering plants to decorate the ceremony and reception sites; you can order fresh flowers directly from the wholesale market and assemble a talented crew of volunteers to do magic with them the day before the wedding; you can order your flowers through a supermarket's floral department; you can purchase (at a very low cost) armloads of peach, apple or cherry blossoms directly from orchard owners; or, finally, you can rent the bulk of the flowers from a wedding supply store. Some brides I know combine several of these ideas, using donated talent and flowers, renting a few showpieces and then purchasing only the bridal bouquet and the two mothers' corsages from a retail florist.

Is it possible for some of the flowers to serve double-duty at the ceremony and reception?

Yes, there are a number of ways you can tactfully and tastefully reuse your flowers. Here are a few:

- Have the ushers quietly carry any floral arrangements, silk or fresh potted plants or trees from the ceremony site to the reception site, using them on the buffet table, cake table, at the corners of the stage, "framing" the bride and groom as they stand under an arch during the reception or placed randomly around the reception hall.

- Design the pew markers so they can double as centerpieces on the tables at the reception.
- Transfer any evergreen or floral garlands from the ceremony site to the reception hall to drape over doorways or windows or along the buffet serving table.
- Use the bride's and bridesmaids' bouquets to form a mound of flowers along the front of the bride's table or to encircle the wedding cake on the cake table.

What size bouquet should I carry? Is there a rule of thumb?

Yes. If you are tall, carry a cascading bouquet; if you're short, carry a smaller one. Also, take your gown into consideration. If it has a lot going on in the way of busy detail, you'll need a simple bouquet that doesn't "fight" with the dress; on the other hand, if your gown is unadorned, with simple, flowing lines, you'll need a more complicated, busier bouquet.

Unfortunately, we need to decorate a huge sanctuary for the ceremony. Any suggestions?

First of all, if money is a problem, you can use free-cut flowering shrubs to fill large wicker baskets. Lilacs work very well, if your wedding happens to be in the spring. Also, remember that it is smart to use white flowers, especially for an evening wedding; they stand out and look larger and brighter than colored flowers. Be sure to embellish the flowers with yards and yards of wide white ribbon, as well. If the ceiling is high, as I imagine your sanctuary's to be, use tall altar flowers—white, of course. My only other suggestion is to drape garlands of greenery and wide white ribbon everywhere possible: along the altar, over the doorways and window frames, from column to column and from pew to pew. This will help tie it all together, and for very little money.

What is a "pull-away boutonniere"?

It is a boutonniere that is concealed inside the bride's bouquet. After the bride is given away by her father at the altar, she removes this pull-away boutonniere and pins it to her groom's lapel as a symbol of her love for him. This can be a touching addition to the ceremony.

What determines the cost of the bride's bouquet?

Here are a few of the factors:

- The ratio of flowers to fillers; the more flowers, the more expensive.
- The price of the flowers you select. If you have your heart set on flowers that are out-of-season or hothouse grown, the cost will go up.
- How the flowers are arranged and whether they are individually wired.
- The overall size of the bouquet; the longer and wider, the more expensive.

If you have a talented amateur florist in your family, you can order all the "ingredients" and have your fresh-flower bouquet made up for about 20 percent of the cost of ordering it through a retail florist. Or one popular idea is to make up the bouquet ahead of time with silk flowers at a similar savings; not only will you avoid last-minute anxieties of working with fresh flowers, but you'll have a treasured momento of your wedding that will stay "fresh" for all the years to come.

What are some alternatives to the traditional bridal bouquet?

You can carry a simple tussy mussy bouquet, a hand-tied arm bouquet of loose fresh flowers, a decorated Bible or prayer book or a lacy white fan decorated with a few silk or fresh flowers.

Lisa Kudrow, one of the stars of the hit television show *Friends*, had a novel idea for her bridal bouquet: She asked her close friends and family members to each bring a different long-stemmed flower hand-selected for her bouquet. The open stems of the eclectic bouquet were tied with a single white satin ribbon, creating a uniquely special, meaningful loose arm arrangement that not only suited the informality of the wedding itself, but the bride's personality as well.

What about my bridal attendants? Are there some clever alternatives for them?

They can carry decorated heart-shaped wreaths, decorated candy canes (really darling for a Christmas wedding, of course), decorated white rabbit's fur muffs, simple sheaves of wheat tied with single ribbons, single candles in beds of flowers, decorated lace parasols or single long-stemmed flowers, each tied with a simple ribbon. If this last idea sounds awfully chintzy, you should know that bridesmaids all over Hollywood are going with the single flower idea. When Teresa Blake (star on *All My Children)* married Mike McGuide (the drummer for the country band Shenandoah), her bridesmaids carried a single white long-stemmed lily, tied with a cluster of trailing white satin ribbons, which were outstanding up against the royal blue of their gowns. When Valerie Bertinelli married Eddie Van Halen, Valerie's bridesmaids carried a single red rose, tied with red and white ribbons, which stood out brilliantly against the women's all-white bridesmaids' gowns. And then there was Wayne Newton's wedding to Kathleen McCrone, where I'm *sure* money was no object, and yet the bridesmaids (dressed in dramatic black floor length gowns) carried simple arm bouquets of a half-dozen white lilies. The point I'm trying to make here is that "less" isn't necessarily synonymous with "cheap." Less can actually be tastefully elegant if it's presented correctly.

Should our mothers' corsages be the same or different according to what they are wearing?

If either mother requests a certain flower or color, be sure to honor her wishes; if the mothers are leaving the decision up to you, however, be *sure* to order identical corsages to avoid any hard feelings.

How soon do I need to book the florist?

As soon as you become engaged, start shopping for a florist. Once you've made your selection, book him or her for your wedding date. However, your actual choice of corsages, bouquets, boutonnieres and decorative arrangements can be made two or three months before the wedding; this will give the florist plenty of time to place any necessary special orders. Most florists book only one or two weddings per weekend, so it's important to be placed on his or her calendar—the detailed order itself can wait.

What is your best word of advice regarding florists?

Stay away from any florist who says, "We'll do whatever you want—just tell us what you have in mind." What you want instead is a florist who is also an *artist*—one who will give *you* ideas and then work with you.

Chapter 18

The Music

What are some of the traditional selections played during the ceremony?

Here is a list of the top 10; however, it should be noted that, unless the ceremony site has restrictions, brides are mixing popular selections with the traditional.

- *The Bridal Chorus* from *Lohengrin* by Wagner ("Here Comes the Bride").
- *Wedding March* by Mendelssohn (for the recessional).
- *Ave Maria* by Schubert.
- *In Thee is Joy* by Bach.
- *Jesu, Joy of Man's Desiring* by Bach.
- *The King of Love My Shepherd Is* by Hinsworth.
- *Joyful, Joyful, We Adore Thee* by Beethoven.
- *Biblical Songs* by Dvorak.
- *The Lord's Prayer* by Malotte.
- *Liebestraum* by Liszt.

What are some of the more popular selections to choose from?

- *Follow Me* by John Denver.
- *We've Only Just Begun,* music by Roger Nichols and lyrics by Paul Williams.
- *Hawaiian Wedding Song* by Al Hoffman and Dick Manning.

- *Wind Beneath My Wings* by Jeff Silbar and Larry Henley.
- *Do You Remember?* by J. Ivanovici.
- *Morning Has Broken* by Eleanor Farjeon.
- *What I Did for Love* by Marvin Hamlisch.
- *All I Ask of You* from "The Phantom of the Opera" by Webber, Hart and Stiltoe.
- *Sunrise, Sunset* from "Fiddler on the Roof" by Harnick and Bock.
- *Evergreen* by Barbra Streisand and Paul Williams.
- *Wedding Song* by Paul Stookey.

What other options are there for the ceremony music?

I've seen the use of children's choirs, adult choirs, stringed trios and quartets, harpsichords, harps, trumpets (especially dramatic when played as a fanfare as the guests rise for the bride's processional), electronic keyboards, solo instruments (flutes, trombones, violins, cellos, french horns, etc.), guitars and even a hand bell choir. Do any of your friends or family members play a musical instrument *well*? (I add *well*, because that is a *must*.) Or do you have a university nearby where you can recruit one or two of their music majors who sing or play instruments *well*?

We would like to hire an orchestra to play for the dancing at our reception, but we would also like some soft background music beforehand. What do you suggest?

Look for an orchestra that can pull out a small string group to play while the guests are eating and visiting. That way, you get two for the price of one.

What are some ways we can cut down on the cost of professional musicians?

The most obvious solution, of course, is to use all the amateur talent available from your friends and relatives, even if it means substituting a flute solo in place of a stringed trio, for example. The next best thing is to supplement any donated talent with a professional, such as the church organist. College and university music departments are also sources of excellent musical talent; call the chairman of the departments to ask for recommendations. Then, of course, there is the simplicity of using pretaped music, especially during the reception. You can actually load up a couple tapes with your favorite music, starting with "your song" for your first dance, followed by others you have personally selected to play throughout the reception. Then, there is also the popular fad of hiring a DJ to play CDs or tapes during the reception; there may even be a teenager in your family who would be thrilled to DJ your reception for free. Note of caution here: Be sure to monitor the selections and the volume of the music.

We think we would like to hire a disc jockey for our reception, instead of a band. Is it possible to find a "classy" DJ, one who will wear a tux and act as a master of ceremonies as well?

Yes, they are out there; the trick is to find a good one. The first thing you should do is ask around; talk to everyone you can find who has recently been married or attended a wedding. Once you've found a couple possibilities, conduct a personal interview so you can get an idea of the person's stage presence, how he will come across to your guests. Also, you will need to explain what you expect in the way of his dress (offer to rent him a tux, if necessary), demeanor, choice of musical selections to be played, volume of the music and his ability to keep things running smoothly in a "classy" way, as you call it.

What are some popular selections for the couple's first dance at the reception?

Here are a few of the favorites:

- *Just the Way You Are* by Billy Joel.
- *I'll Always Love You* by Taylor Dane.

- *Unforgettable* by Irving Gordon.
- *Wonderful Tonight* by Eric Clapton.
- *Looking Through the Eyes of Love* by Marvin Hamlisch and Carole Bayer Sager.
- *Can You Feel the Love Tonight?* by Elton John and Tim Rice.
- *Love Will Keep Us Together* by Neil Sedaka.
- *All I Ask of You* from "The Phantom of the Opera" by Webber, Hart and Stiltoe.
- *Stand By Me* by Ben E. King.
- *Endless Love* by Diana Ross and Lionel Richie.
- *We've Only Just Begun* lyrics by Paul Williams and music by Roger Nichols.

Are there any special songs for the father-daughter dance or the mother-son dance? Or does it really matter?

It has become quite trendy to select specific songs for these traditional dances. Here are some of the songs being used these days:

For the father-daughter dance:

- *My Heart Belongs to Daddy* by Cole Porter.
- *Sunrise, Sunset* from "Fiddler on the Roof" by Harnick and Bock.
- *Thank Heaven for Little Girls* from "Gigi" by Lerner and Loewe.
- *My Girl* by Smokey Robinson and Ronald White.
- *The Times of Your Life* by Paul Anka.

For the mother-son dance:

- *You Are the Sunshine of My Life* by Stevie Wonder.
- *Wind Beneath My Wings* by Larry Henley and Jeff Silbar.
- *Summer Wind* by Mayer and Mercer.
- *You're the Top* by Cole Porter.
- *My Mother's Eyes* by Gilbert and Baer.

What are some of the ethnic numbers usually played for the guests to dance to?

Here are the most common choices:

Jewish:	*Mitzvah Tentzel* and *The Horah* (to the tune of *Havah Nagila*)
Spanish-Mexican:	*Celito Lindo*
Greek:	*Kalamatiano* (to the tune of *Samiotisa*) and *The Handkerchief Dance*
Italian:	*Tarantella*
Scottish:	*The Highland Fling*
Irish:	*The Irish Jig*

Is there some simple way to audition a band before we actually hire them to play at our reception?

There are several things you can do:

- Ask if you can eavesdrop on their next wedding gig. (You won't need long to decide whether they will work for you or not.)
- Ask to hear one of their audition tapes, either audio or video.
- Ask for references.
- Talk to staff people at other reception sites who have heard the band play; also, talk to your caterer or bridal consultant.

What is the average cost of a DJ?

Depending on your part of the country, DJs run from $250 to $750.

How about the average cost of a live band?

The cost of a live band not only depends on your part of the country, but on the size, quality and reputation of the band itself; you'll find bands ranging all the way from $500 to $10,000.

Is there a rule of thumb on how big the band should be?

Many experts say one musician for every 25 guests, with a minimum of four. It has been my personal observation that it depends a great deal on the quality of the sound system: I've heard three and four piece bands that had a "big band" sound. By the way, in case you want a big band sound, but your reception hall is small, you might have them play "unplugged."

Chapter 19

The Transportation

What transportation do we need to provide?

Every wedding is different, depending on how many out-of-towners need transportation, the proximity of the ceremony and reception sites and how many vehicles are being furnished by friends and family, but here is a list of the basics: transportation for the bride and her father from her home to the ceremony site; transportation for the mother of the bride and the bride's attendants; transportation for the groom's parents; transportation for the groom and his attendants; and transportation for the bride and groom from the ceremony to the reception.

Often one limousine and driver may be hired to serve double-duty: carrying the bride and her father to the ceremony and then carrying the bride and groom from the ceremony to the reception. Of course, the couple will also need a "getaway" vehicle.

We would like to have champagne served in our limo on the ride from the ceremony to the reception. Can the limousine service provide this?

Only if they're licensed to do so. Check with them ahead of time. It may be that if you furnish your own iced bucket of champagne, along with a couple of long-stemmed champagne glasses, your driver will be allowed to serve you.

How can we locate a horse-drawn carriage?

Look in your yellow pages under *wedding services* or *carriages*. When you locate a company that rents carriages, be sure to ask them whether they furnish liability insurance and a uniformed, white-gloved driver.

Do you have any suggestions for a clever getaway vehicle? We want something creative that will be cute in the photos.

There are dozens of unique alternatives to the standard limo. Here are just a few: horse and buggy, fire truck, school bus, antique car, bicycle-built-for-two, hot air balloon, dogsled, sleigh, ski gondola, speedboat, trolley, cable car, snowmobile, sailboat, hay wagon, little red tractor, helicopter or any convertible. Not only do these make for cute photos, but they're also fun to decorate.

With all the weddings you attend, have you seen any cute decorations for the couple's getaway vehicle?

I think I've seen it all! Here are some of the more "photogenic" ideas I've seen lately:

- Photo poster. As the couple drives off, it's really cute to have their photo, on an oversized poster, attached to the back of the car, surrounded by crepe paper ribbons, flowers and so on. Take any photo or negative to your local drug store photo department and have them blow it up into a poster.
- A "stop sign" made out of poster board, bordered with red lettering in the center that has the couple's names or "God Bless the Newlyweds."
- A bouquet of flowers tied to the hood ornament with streaming ribbons floating down.
- Balloons, tissue bells, pompoms or bows made out of tulle netting, all in the wedding's colors.

- Use a "Just Married" car kit, which can be purchased from your local wedding or party supply store, to write choice sayings along the side of the car.
- Cans, shoes or vocational novelties. In addition to the traditional cans and shoes, trail along any novelty items that denote the couple's hobbies or occupations, such as school books wrapped tightly with a narrow belt, old stethoscopes, golf clubs, etc. Along with these novelties, you can add a couple of posters that read: "This One's Sold," for the groom who sells real estate, or "Gonna' Be a Three-Alarm Fire Tonight," if the groom is a fireman, for example. If you put on your thinking cap you can think up something clever for almost any occupation or hobby.
- Giant doves or hearts. Make doves or double overlapping hearts out of poster board, outline them with crepe paper flowers, pompoms, etc. You can write the couple's names inside the hearts.

There are no rules when it comes to decorating the getaway vehicle, so let your mind go crazy. To give you an idea of what I mean, an old rusty Jeep was decorated for one wedding I attended, wrapped with crepe paper and decorated with flowers, balloons and ribbons, roll bar and all. The old jeep turned into a "wedding float" that led the way through town after the reception, followed by the rest of the honking, cheering party. No one would have guessed there was an old Jeep under there! In another case, the entire wedding party hiked up onto a horse-drawn wagon full of hay and partied through town until the bridal couple was finally dropped off at the airport. Think of the resources available to you, and see if you can come up with an original idea of your own.

Are there any precautions when it comes to decorating the vehicle?

Here are a few tips:

- Don't use glue, cellophane tape, rubber cement or regular paint of any kind.
- If you're going to decorate with fresh flowers, choose hardy varieties, not "wimpy" flowers that will wilt in the weather, such as tulips, camelias or gardenias.
- Keep the windshield clear. Don't write on it or drape it with anything.
- If there's any chance at all for rain, ditch your crepe paper ideas. Colored crepe paper will "bleed" all over the car and may cause permanent stains.

We've heard some horrible tales about limo drivers who arrived late or drunk or limos that were filthy. How can we avoid such a disaster?

Your best bet is to find a limousine company that belongs to the National Limousine Association. If you can't locate one, call this association at 800-NLA-7007.

How much do limos run per hour?

From $25 to $200 per hour, usually with a three hour minimum.

Are there more affordable alternatives?

One couple rented a Lincoln Town Car at $39.95 for the entire day; another rented an antique red trolley car, complete with uniformed driver, at a total cost of $100 for the day.

Chapter 20

All Those Extras

What about ceremony programs? Are they necessary?

They are optional, but much appreciated by your guests, especially those who don't know the members of the wedding party.

What about printed thank-you notes, with something really personal, such as, "Ron and I sincerely thank you for your lovely gift"?

Actually, your suggested wording isn't at all personal; in fact, by the very nature of it being a preprinted thank-you note, you have lost any hope of it being a personalized response. Sorry, but thank-you notes must be in your own handwriting.

Is it all right if I get help writing my thank-you notes? We expect to have more than 200 gifts.

Your thank-you notes should be in your own handwriting, although it's fine if your husband helps you with them, particularly to his own friends and family. Remember one thing: No matter which one of you writes the thank-you note, be sure to reference the other. For example, "Jim and I really appreciate the..."

I was hoping there wouldn't be a lot of children running around at my wedding, but several people in the wedding party have small children. Should we provide child care?

Strictly speaking, rules of etiquette say that small children should not be invited to weddings. In the real world, however, there usually seem to be several running around. At one wedding I attended there were about 10 children playing hide-and-seek in the garden where the reception was being held. I cringed as I watched the flower beds turn to "mulch" and the flower girls' dresses turn into instant play clothes. How much better if there would have been a couple of teenagers on hand to play games with these children, or show them videos, or *something*! For your own peace of mind, I definitely recommend providing child care.

What about lodging for the wedding party and all those who are coming in from out of town?

The bride should make the arrangements for her attendants and the groom for his. If they can't be put up with relatives and friends, you will need to reserve and pay for their hotel or motel rooms. As far as the other guests or family members who are coming in from out of town, they will be expected to pay for their own lodging, although they may request that you make their reservations.

Our reception is being held at a large downtown hotel that charges for parking. Wouldn't it be all right for the guests to pay for their own parking, or are we expected to pick up that tab?

Unfortunately, you are. It isn't nice to invite guests to your wedding and expect them to pay for anything.

We expect to have quite a few relatives who will fly in for the wedding; will my parents be expected to feed them after the reception?

If a full meal was served at the reception, the relatives may be invited over to your home for a light dessert and coffee after the reception, more for the purpose of visiting than of eating. However, if the reception consisted only of finger foods or dessert, your mother may wish to serve them a meal or, better yet, treat them to a meal at a restaurant, where they can all visit without the extra work.

What are some of the little hidden expenses that usually pop up at the last minute?

Here are some of the extras you need to think about:

- **A guest book and pen.** If it is a large wedding, you may want to provide two books, one at each door as the guests enter the reception. Then it's also a good idea to have one of your helpers walk around once the reception is under way and ask the guests if they have signed the book. An economical alternative to the standard white guest book is a long piece of off-white parchment; roll it tightly into a scroll, then let it unwind, creating an attractive and unusual record of your guests. After the wedding this scroll can then be kept as a momento by rewinding it and tying with a ribbon or by framing it. One bride provided sheets of paper along with crayons and felt tip markets for the guests to write messages or draw pictures—a truly unique alternative to the traditional guest book. One more clever idea: Have your guests sign the matting around your engagement photo (on display during the reception).

- **Decorated baskets for the reception.** You will need two or more decorated baskets for distributing the favors and collecting any gift envelopes the guests may bring to the reception.

- **Toasting glasses for the bride and groom.** You can purchase decorated champagne glasses engraved with the names of the couple, or you can purchase them from a factory outlet store and decorate them yourself for a fraction of the cost.

- **Cake cutting knife and server.** You can purchase them in a set, engraved or decorated or, as with the toasting glasses, purchase them at an outlet store and decorate them yourself. A popular sentimental alternative these days is to use your mother's or grandmother's, decorated or not.
- **The bride's throwaway bouquet.** The bride usually wants to keep and preserve her bouquet and has a "pretend" one made up to throw away at the reception. You can have an inexpensive duplicate made up by your florist, or you can assemble one yourself out of fresh or silk flowers. The silk idea is best because you can make it up ahead of time and forget about it.
- **The bride's garters.** The bride will need two—one to keep as a momento and one to be tossed by her groom.
- **The bride's gifts to her bridal attendants**, such as a pearl necklace, pair of earrings, bracelet, picture frame, silver spoon, pair of gloves, heart-shaped locket, compact, scarf or jewelry box. For her flower girl or junior attendants she will also want to provide a thoughtful gift, such as a Barbie doll, a tea set, stuffed animals or a book.
- **The groom's gifts to his attendants**, such as a pen and pencil set, key chain, wallet, Swiss army knife (a very popular choice these days), money clip, travel kit, comb and brush set or tie clasp. For the boys he may want to give a train set, stuffed animal, book or electronic game.
- **The couple's gifts to the helpers.** The couple will want to give thoughtful thank-you gifts to everyone who helped out in any way during the ceremony and the reception—from the guest book attendants, to the cake servers, to the host and hostess, to all those who weren't paid professionals. Here are some suggestions: a framed photo of the

bride and groom or of the wedding invitation, a gift
certificate, perfume or cologne, tickets to a sporting
event or concert, a silver plate or bowl or a crystal
vase or paperweight.

- **The couple's gifts to their parents.** It is
traditional for the bride and groom to give their
parents keepsakes or momentos of the wedding,
to be treasured by them always. Here are a few
ideas: a framed poem or thank-you note; a double
frame containing the couple's photo on one side
and the wedding invitation on the other; a live
tree that can be planted in the parent's yard as a
reminder of the wedding; a wedding memory silk
topiary tree for their home which contains
momentos of the wedding, such as actual pieces of
ribbon or dried flowers from the bride's bouquet,
one of the favors, tufts of fabric from the
bridesmaids' gowns, plus a tiny photo of the bride
and groom.

- **Last-minute alterations.** From the time you
purchase or rent the gown or tuxedo, you may
lose or gain weight, so it's not unusual to have
last-minute alterations. The bride, in fact, can
easily drop five pounds the week before the
wedding.

- **Sheet music for the musicians.** Be prepared to
purchase the sheet music for the pieces you have
selected for your ceremony and reception. When
our daughter was married, she was determined to
use the wedding march from *The Sound of Music*
for the recessional after the ceremony, but the
organist had never heard of it. We had difficulty
finding it, as a matter of fact, and finally had it
specially ordered.

- **Aisle runner.** I'm not crazy about these things
myself because they tend to "bunch up" as the
bride walks down the aisle, plus the fact that it is
very difficult to find a white aisle runner that

matches the white in the bride's gown. If you definitely want to use one, however, it can be rented from a wedding supply store.

- **A kneeling pillow** (for the bride and groom to kneel on at the altar). It is a nice tradition to embroider your names and wedding date on a white or ivory pillow; then, pass it down to your children and grandchildren to use someday in their weddings, with their names and wedding dates embroidered under yours.

- **Makeup artist, manicurist and hair stylist.** Many brides these days hire one of each to be on hand the morning of the wedding to beautify the bride and her attendants. If you're lucky, you have some talented friends who can help out.

- **Child care.** As I've already mentioned, according to proper wedding etiquette small children shouldn't be invited to the wedding, but in the real world you can expect to have quite a few running around. That's why I recommend hiring a few teenagers to help out.

- **Calligrapher.** Here is one of those extra expenses that can really get out of hand if you decide to have a calligrapher address all the invitations and enclosure cards. An alternative is to purchase a black calligraphy pen and do them yourself. By taking it nice and slow and adding a few twirls and loops, you can fake it pretty well.

- **Rental of awnings or tents**, especially in case of rain.

- **Rental of tables, chairs, fountains, lattice arches or portable bars.**

- **Security officer** (see Chapter 15).

- **House sitter** to stay at your home during the ceremony and reception. (Remember that burglars read the wedding announcements in the newspaper, too.)

What kind of tips will we be expected to pay for all the services?

Unless the tip is already included in your caterer's bill, you will need to add 15 to 20 percent of the total. Also, expect to tip the parking attendants, coatroom attendant and powder room attendants, if there are any. Finally, be prepared to tip the limo driver 10 to 15 percent.

When should I buy the marriage license?

Every state has different requirements, so your first step is to call the county clerk's office and ask how to proceed. You will need to know the length of the waiting period, whether a blood test is required and what you need to bring in the way of identification. Make this call as soon as you become engaged because time has a way of sneaking up on you, and this is the most common last-minute snafu in couples' wedding plans—putting the marriage license off until the last minute.

What are other types of marriage certificates that may be required?

Your church will probably provide a marriage certificate for you to sign, often a lovely momento suitable for framing. In the Jewish faith there is also a traditional *Ketubah*, the Orthodox or Conservative Jewish marriage contract that is an agreement spelling out the groom's responsibilities toward his bride. The Iranian wedding certificate contains the traditional Persian wedding covenant and is beautifully decorated with birds, flowers and Islamic symbols. The Quakers, Amish and Mennonites also have their own traditional marriage certificates, some of which are signed by all the guests present.

What's a "wedding newsletter"?

This is a really trendy new thing to send out to everyone involved in the wedding—the members of the wedding party, family members and close friends. It's a fun little letter that goes out periodically to keep everyone informed of the plans in progress, introduce them to each other by giving biographical sketches of each person and tell them about hotel accommodations, airport shuttle services available, plans for the rehearsal dinner and any special events or activities planned.

Is there some kind of short-term insurance we can buy that will cover our wedding gifts?

Yes, there is. You can purchase a rider to your existing homeowner's or renter's insurance policy that will protect the value of your wedding gifts. This rider is very affordable and provides great peace of mind.

What about "wedding insurance"?

Wedding insurance covers nonrefundable expenses in case of a canceled wedding (heaven forbid!). It also covers such things as photography mishaps and personal liability should a guest be injured at the wedding or reception. Fireman's Fund Insurance Company has been providing these insurance policies for many years, but check with your favorite company and compare rates.

What is an "afterglow"?

An *afterglow* is another party; it may follow the reception or be held the next day. The purpose of this informal party is to entertain family and out-of-town guests; often the bride and groom attend this party (although I always wonder why they don't have something better to do!). Anyway, this informal gathering may include anything from a breakfast to a brunch to a barbecue around the pool to "High Tea in the Garden." It is a chance for everyone to relax and reminisce about the wedding.

What is a "guest basket"?

It is a basket made up ahead of time as a welcome gift for out-of-town wedding guests staying at hotels. Each basket contains a schedule of the wedding festivities, transportation arrangements, a map of the area, brochures on local places of interest, along with fresh fruit, a bottle of champagne or wine and a personal note welcoming each guest.

Chapter 21

The Honeymoon

In addition to money for the transportation, accommodations and meals, what are the other funds we will need to budget for our honeymoon?

Allow for local transportation, your entertainment, tips, momentos, impulse spending and, most important of all, a nice little emergency fund. Part of your emergency fund may be a couple $100 bills folded away inside your wallet and the other part may be in the form of savings back home, accessible with your ATM card at your honeymoon destination. The biggest budget shock for most honeymooners is how fast they run out of the pocket money needed for tips, little gifts for each other, honeymoon momentos and unexpected expenses.

What are the most popular honeymoon destinations?

Newlyweds traditionally love any destination that has a beach, including Florida, Hawaii, Mexico and the Caribbean. They also swarm to the couples-only honeymoon resorts, especially in the Poconos. Another choice is to take a cruise, with Mexican and Caribbean cruises being the most popular. Other popular destinations are Hilton Head Island, South Carolina, Las Vegas, San Diego, San Antonio, Disney World in Florida and Vail or Breckenridge, Colorado.

We will only have a week for our honeymoon, but we have our hearts set on Hawaii. Do you think a week will be long enough, with the travel time and all?

This is a matter of opinion, of course, but the only way I think it will work is if you're already on the West Coast. Even so, by the time you get to the airport, park your car, check in and make the five-hour flight from San Francisco to Hawaii, you've lost a whole day, which means that your seven days is already down to five by the time you settle into your hotel. Why not save the Hawaii trip for your first anniversary and honeymoon someplace closer to home—say, no more than a three- or four-hour *drive* to your destination?

This wedding is costing us a fortune, especially since our parents are going through financial problems right now and aren't able to help us, which means we will have to squeeze our honeymoon out of whatever money we have left over. Any suggestions?

For less than $600 you can rent or borrow a self-contained RV and park it alongside a lake or stream, or your state probably has some quiet, romantic spot where you can rent a little cabin or stay at a bed-and-breakfast. For about $1,000 you can do something a little more exotic, depending on where you live. If you live in Arizona or Southern California, for example, you can afford a three-night cruise out of Los Angeles with stops at Catalina, Ensenada and Cabo San Lucas, or if you live in the Southeast and can drive to Miami, there are also short, affordable cruises available to the Caribbean. The Poconos also offer total honeymoon packages for less than $1,000, depending on how many nights you stay. You may want to pick up a copy of my book entitled *How to Have a Fabulous, Romantic Honeymoon on a Budget* which has hundreds of other affordable honeymoon ideas. In any case, remember this important fact: It's *who* you're with that counts and *any* destination looks pretty good when you're filled with that "newlywed love."

What's so great about the Poconos? I've heard about them for years.

The resorts located in the Pocono Mountains of Pennsylvania, as well as the other couples-only destination resorts around the country and in the Caribbean, cater to honeymooners. These resorts absolutely drip with sensuality, with their deep, heart-shaped Whirlpool tubs, private swimming pools, velvet-draped canopied beds, candlelit dinners and romantic musical entertainment. The packages are all-inclusive, which means that everything is included in one price, such as the lodging, food, entertainment and dozens of activities and amenities. Call 1-800-POCONOS for free honeymoon information.

What do we do if we should lose our airline tickets during our honeymoon?

One precaution would be to book with one of the airlines now offering "ticketless flying." That way you have nothing to lose in the first place. Otherwise, contact the travel agent or airline through which you made the reservations. It may (1) reissue new tickets or (2) require that you purchase new tickets until you file for a refund after you return from the trip.

We would like to find a romantic destination for our honeymoon that we can have all to ourselves, without thousands of other honeymooners everywhere we look. Do you have any suggestions?

Well, if you like the outdoors and your idea of a romantic setting is watching the setting sun reflect on the lake in front of your secluded log cabin, you might want to consider a wilderness honeymoon. Some of the national parks offer incredible honeymoon settings, such as Jenny Lake or

Jackson Lake in the Grand Teton National Park in Wyoming, or you may want to consider a remote guest ranch, such as those hidden away in the mountains of Colorado. Pick up a copy of Gene Gilgore's *Ranch Vacations* for specific destinations.

What are some other ways we can save money on our honeymoon?

The best way by far is to establish a gift registry at a travel agency. That way your friends and relatives can contribute toward your honeymoon in lieu of a wedding gift. Another idea is to rent a condo, private home, RV or houseboat at your destination, instead of a pricey hotel. You'll have more room and privacy for half the price. When it comes to meals, there are several ways to save: Make lunch your main meal of the day, rather than dinner; eat off the appetizer menu instead of the regular menu; take a picnic to some secluded, romantic spot (be sure to register for a picnic basket and insulated cooler when you're setting up your gift registries); split a meal once in a while (a Mexican fajita, a pizza or a Chinese meal, for example); fill up for free at a happy hour buffet where the food is free for the price of a couple of drinks; and, finally, look for hotels, motels and, of course, bed-and-breakfasts, where the breakfast is included in the price.

What is the most affordable honeymoon you've ever heard of?

Well, other than a free honeymoon through a travel agency gift registry, the most affordable idea is to honeymoon at home. This takes some very creative planning, such as:

- Tell everyone you're flying to Hawaii for your honeymoon.
- Don't tell a *soul* you're honeymooning in your own apartment or home—not even your parents, best man or maid of honor!

- A few days before the wedding, stock your home with plenty of food (preferably prepared food) and drinks, paper plates, cups, plastic champagne glasses, candles (lots and lots of them!), romantic CDs and tapes, bubble bath, massage oil, a *huge* supply of sheets and towels, fresh strawberries, several boxes of chocolates, your favorite cologne and perfume and a couple dozen movies on video (not that you'll *really* watch them, of course).

- Bring packed suitcases with you to the reception that can be placed (in full view of your guests) into the trunk of your getaway vehicle to convince them you're really flying off somewhere!

- Be sure you aren't followed home after your reception. If necessary, head for the airport and stay on that route until you've ditched the last of the wedding party who may be following you.

- Once you're home, hide your car in the garage, unplug the telephone and don't answer the door— *no matter what!*

We're worried about our luggage getting lost by the airlines; is it safer to check it curbside at the airport or inside at the airline's ticket counter?

Industry-wide, only four bags are mishandled for every 1,000 passengers, but I can't find statistics on whether these four bags were checked at curbside or at the counter. To minimize your risk of loss in any case, here are some rules to follow:

- Be sure your bags are tagged well with your name, address and telephone number. Tear off all other tags from previous trips.

- Make copies of your itinerary and place one *inside* each piece of luggage—that way your bags have a better chance of catching up with you at your honeymoon destination.

- Make sure the three-letter airport code placed on your bag corresponds with your destination.

What if the airline loses our luggage after all?

Fill out a lost-luggage form with the airline at its customer service office at the airport; most lost luggage isn't really lost at all, only delayed, and will probably arrive on the next flight from your origination city. You may want to hang around the airport and wait for that flight in the hopes that your luggage will be there; otherwise, you can go ahead to your hotel and the airlines will have your luggage delivered directly to you as soon as it does arrive. Even with all the flying I've done through the years, an airline has never lost my luggage for good—it has always come in on a later flight. Meanwhile, it's smart to carry as much luggage on board as the airline allows—usually one medium suitcase or garment bag per person, plus one smaller case or bag. Be sure your on-board luggage carries all the essentials: toothbrush, toothpaste, razor, makeup, contraceptives, medicines, a nightie, one change of underwear, an extra set of contact lenses, jewelry, camera, traveler's checks, passports, tickets, etc.

I've had situations when I've been traveling on business where a hotel doesn't have a room available after all, even though I have a confirmation number. How can I avoid this happening on our honeymoon?

First of all, have your best man call a few days ahead of time to confirm your reservations. Then, if you arrive and the reservation clerk tries to give you the run-around, ask to speak to the manager and tell him or her you are on your honeymoon (*always* tell everyone you're on your honeymoon, which will give you "freebies," upgrades and excellent service) and that your room was paid for in advance or guaranteed with your credit card. Be sure you have a written confirmation with you, not just a confirmation number. Then it will be up to the manager to provide you with a room, which will usually be a substantial upgrade. If the hotel is completely out of rooms, the manager must find you comparable accommodations in some other hotel nearby.

How much cash should we take with us on our honeymoon? Or should it all be in traveler's checks?

Be sure to have some cash on you, at least $200, preferably in small bills, which are handy for tipping. The rest of your money should be in the form of traveler's checks, also in small denominations because many establishments balk at anything $50 on up. By the way, keep a list of your traveler's checks' numbers, as well as your credit card numbers and checking account numbers, separate from the checks and cards themselves. If you're traveling overseas, be sure to convert some cash into the foreign currency *before* you leave on your honeymoon. For emergency money, keep a little hidden away in your carry-on luggage (a couple hundred dollars), plus be prepared to use your ATM card at your destination if you should run short of cash.

What is the "honeymoon squeeze"?

Well, it's not good, I can tell you that! The *honeymoon squeeze* is where one thief engages you in conversation or bumps into you to distract you while his accomplice picks your pocket or steals your luggage. These thieves pick on honeymooners because they think they'll be easy prey; they usually hang out at airports, but be careful wherever you go!

What is your best word of advice to us as far as planning our honeymoon?

My best advice for you is to delay your departure for a day or two after the wedding; stay in the honeymoon suite of one of the nicer hotels in your city. This will give you time to catch your breath and get a little rest before you actually leave on your honeymoon. Too often the couple leaves the wedding reception at midnight and tries to make it to the airport for an overnight flight or, worse yet, tries to drive all the way to their honeymoon destination.

How long should a honeymoon be?

Although most honeymoons are only seven to 10 days long, most of the couples I've talked with agree that a honeymoon should be a minimum of two weeks. They think anything less than that goes by too fast and isn't restful enough after all the months of stress and planning. A poll taken by *Bride's* magazine showed that the average length of a honeymoon was nine days.

What is the average cost of a honeymoon?

According to the same *Bride's* magazine poll, the average honeymoon cost was $3,200.

Do you have any tips for packing for the honeymoon?

Packing for a two-week honeymoon is no simple task. Here are a few ideas that can make it easier:

- First of all, make a detailed list of *everything* you will need to pack.
- Allow an entire morning or afternoon to pack.
- Open your suitcases and hanging garment bag in front of you on a bed.
- Start with the heavy items: books, shoes, hair dryer, etc. (Wrap your shoes in plastic bags.)
- Next, fill in around these heavy items with your soft, crushable clothing, such as T-shirts, underwear, nightgowns, jeans, etc. (Roll them up tight to keep them from wrinkling.)
- Now you're ready for your blouses, shirts, slacks, dresses, shorts, etc. (Lay tissue paper between each item as you fold it into the suitcase.)

What are the "honeymoon blues"?

These are the blues that sometimes follow the letdown after the excitement and exhaustion of the wedding and its preceding months of preparation. They are nothing to worry about! They are common! Many honeymoon couples have them! The best cures are to:

- Share your feelings with your new spouse.
- Stay as busy as possible on your honeymoon (add a few extra sports activities or excursions to your itinerary).
- Talk about your future and all the fun things you will do: with your gifts, with your friends, with each other.
- Try to get some rejuvenating sleep and rest.

Fortunately, this mini-depression only lasts a couple of days, if you experience it at all.

How do we go about applying for passports?

First, ask your travel agent if passports are required for your destination. If they are, begin early with the application process; it can take two or three months. You can apply for your passports at county clerk's offices, certain authorized post offices and any federal passport office. You will need to bring your proof of citizenship (your birth or naturalization certificate), proof of identity (driver's license), two identical 2- x 2-inch head-shot photographs and money to pay the passport fee (about $42).

When my husband and I recently tried to renew our passports, which we obtained originally with no hassle at all, we discovered that my husband's official birth certificate (which was acceptable when his first passport was issued) was no longer considered "official" enough, so we went through several months of unbelievable red tape to go back through Alameda County's archives to retrieve his birth certificate so that an officially certified, acceptable copy could be made. The moral of this story is that you shouldn't assume it's easy to get a passport—it isn't always, so start early!

After going through all that, what if we lose our passports?

First, report the loss to your nearest U.S. embassy and follow their instructions. It will be helpful to them if you know your passport number, date and place of issue (keep this information separate from your passport when you start out on your trip). Many seasoned travelers keep a photocopy of their passport packed separately, of course. But please don't lose your passports!

Should my fiancee apply for her passport in her married name?

No, you won't be able to do that. She will need to apply for her passport in her maiden name, which will work out fine because it will still be legal once she's married. Just be sure her airline ticket is in her maiden name because it is imperative that the names on her ticket and passport match.

How can we stay healthy on our honeymoon?

Here are some suggestions:

- Pack a portable medicine "chest" that contains: all your regular prescription medicines, additional prescription medicines in case of nausea, allergies, motion sickness and urinary-tract infections, insect repellents, cold remedies, and antibacterial ointment and spray.
- If you're traveling to a foreign country, such as Mexico, don't drink the water. Don't even chew the ice! Drink only bottled water, sodas or other bottled beverages.
- Bring plenty of sunscreen—and use it!

What about tipping on our honeymoon? I don't know how much to tip for each service.

I'm a great believer in tipping on the merit system. If someone gives me great service, I think they deserve a great tip; on the other hand, if I'm treated poorly or ignored, I may leave nothing at all. But assuming you'll have at least acceptable service everywhere you go, here are some tipping guidelines:

Airport porter	$1 per bag
Ship cabin or dining room stewards	$3 per day, per person
Hotel bellboy	$1 per bag, plus a dollar or two more for extra service (giving you directions to restaurants, etc.)
Waiter or waitress	15 percent of the bill
Hotel chambermaid	$5 per couple, per week
Taxi driver	15 percent of the bill
Golf caddie	25 percent of his fee
Tour guide	$5 per couple

Do you have any cost-cutting tips for us while we're on our honeymoon?

Here are several tips that can save you a chunk of money:

- If you are honeymooning in a foreign country, don't exchange money at your hotel—go to a local bank instead.
- Be sure to pack plenty of film, toothpaste, shampoo and suntan lotion, the four things most likely to need replacing at your honeymoon site where they will cost much more than at your discount drugstore back home.

- Ask the locals for good, but inexpensive, places to eat—if you go the four-star route every night you'll run out of spending money real fast!
- Don't even *think* of touching the minibar.
- Find out if tipping is the norm; in some countries the service charges are already built into the menu prices!
- Don't phone home—too expensive, especially from your hotel room where they may tack on a per-call service charge.
- Always take advantage of the complimentary breakfast offered by your hotel; even if it's continental, it will at least pacify you until lunch.
- Use public transportation or your hotel's shuttle service as much as possible—avoid the high cost of a taxi.
- Don't get carried away and buy more than you can bring back through customs *without* paying duty.
- Do a lot of free (but romantic) things, such as taking a mountain hike, collecting shells along the beach, etc.
- Tell *everyone* you're on your honeymoon—you'll be surprised how many freebies this news will bring!

Epilogue

I hope my answers will help you have the most wonderful wedding day possible, one that reflects your personal blend of creativity, fun and, most of all, love. As I leave you now, here are my last words of advice:

- Don't worry if *everything* doesn't turn out perfectly—every wedding has some little thing that goes wrong, but don't let it throw you. It's not worth it!
- Keep a sense of humor.
- Take good care of yourself between now and the wedding—remember those relaxation techniques?
- Smile and enjoy your wedding day!

****

When it's all over and you're back from your honeymoon, I'd love to hear from you. Tell me all about your day and if you happen to have an extra wedding photo, please send it along. Write me in care of my publisher:

Career Press
P.O. Box 687
Franklin Lakes, NJ 07417

Index

Addressing invitations, 54-55
After the reception, 133-134
Afterglow, 36, 170
Airline tickets, losing, 175
Aisle runner, 108, 167-168
Alcohol, at reception, 131
All-night wedding, 36-37
Alterations, 64, 167
American Gem Society, 18
Announcements,
  engagement, 14-15, 55
Anxiety, 69-70, 72, 75
Appraisal, engagement ring, 18
Arch-of-steel ceremony, 101
Association of Bridal
  Consultants, 32-33
Attendants
  bride's, 79-81
  groom's, 83-84

Bachelor party, 73, 77
Ballerina veil, 67
Band, for reception, 157-158
Bands, gold wedding, 19, 21-23
Bell ringers, 105-106
Best man, duties of, 83, 124
Black and white theme, 90-91
Blusher veil, 67
Bouquet, 126, 132, 149-151, 166

Boutonniere, 150
Bridal attendants, 79-81
  flowers for, 151
Bridal consultant, 31-34
Bridal gown, 61-71
Bridal Guide, 69
Bridal registry, 39-43
Bridal salon, 69
Bridal show, 70
Bridal veil, 62-63, 66-67
Bride, 61-72
Bride's family's expenses, 46-47
Bride's magazine, 180
Bridesmaids
  flowers for, 151
  gowns for, 80-81, 84
  luncheon for, 80
Budget wedding, 49
Bustling, on bridal gown, 71

Cake, 115, 121-122, 129-131
  dummy wedding, 127-128
  Fairmont presentation, 122
  groom's, 121
  toppers, 128-129
Calligrapher, 168
Camera, disposable, 142-143
Candid photo shots, 139-140

Candles, 104, 109

Cash, for honeymoon, 179

Cash bar, at reception, 115, 131

Caterers, 117, 120-121

Cathedral veil, 67

Catholic service, 107

Ceremony, 99-109
  arch-of-steel, 101
  fainting during, 102
  flowers at, 147-152
  intimate, 101
  music for, 153-154
  photographs during, 136
  programs for, 163
  religious, 28, 99, 101ff
  unity candle, 109
  videotaping, 141

Certificates, marriage, 169

Champagne, 123-124, 159

Chapel veil, 67

Children, including, 34, 164, 168

Christmas theme, 91

Church ceremony, 99, 101ff

Civil ceremony, 100, 103-104
  invitation for, 54

Consultant, bridal, 31-34

Contract, photography, 136-137

Coordinator, wedding, 31-32

Costs, wedding, 45-49

Costume wedding, 37

Cup, marriage, 116

Dance order, reception, 119-120

Dances, music for, 155-157

Date of wedding, 27, 29

Decorations, 89-94, 160-162, 165

Destination wedding, 34-36

Destinations, honeymoon, 173ff

Diamond ring, 17-20

Diaries, wedding day, 115

Dinner, rehearsal, 96-98

Disc jockey, 155, 157

Divorce, wearing rings before, 23

Divorced parents, 53, 85-87, 120, 136

Dog, as part of ceremony, 37

Down payment on house, 43

Dummy wedding cake, 127-128

Eloping, 33

"Emergency kit," bridal, 65-66

Enclosure cards, 56-57

Engagement period, 13-15

Engraving invitations, 51, 55

Engraving wedding rings, 21

Ethnic theme, 89-90, 117, 157

Expense
  hidden, 165-168
  of bridal gown, 64-65, 68-69
  of cake, 127-130
  of flowers, 147ff
  of honeymoon, 173ff
  of music, 154-155, 157
  of photography, 144-146
  of reception, 113, 131-132
  of transportation, 162
  tipping, 169, 183
  wedding, 18, 45-49

Extras, 163-171

Fainting during ceremony, 102

Fairmont cake presentation, 122

Father-daughter dance, music for, 156

Fathers' attire, 87

Favors, wedding, 118-119

Fingertip veil, 67

Fireworks, at reception, 133

First dance, music for, 155-156
Fit of wedding rings, 23
Florists, advice regarding, 152
Flower girl, 80
Flowers, 147-152
Food, at reception, 114-117
   listing on invitation, 59
Foreign country, wedding in, 35
Formal photo shots, 138-139
Formal wedding, 74, 113-114
   invitation for, 52
Formality, of wedding, 27-28
"Four Cs," of diamonds, 19-20
French marriage cup, 116
French service, at reception, 124

Garden wedding, 93
Garters, 132, 166
"Getaway" vehicle, 159-162
Gift registry, 58
Gifts
   damaged, 43
   displaying at reception, 123
   duplicate, 43
   guarding at reception, 132
   insurance for, 170
   opening at reception, 122
   to attendants, 166
   to helpers, 166-167
   to parents, 167
   wedding, 39-43
Giving away a bride, 28, 85
Gown, bridal, 61-71, 80
Gowns, bridesmaids', 80-81, 84
Groom, 73-77
Groom registry, 42-43
Groom's attendants, 83-84
Groom's cake, 121
Groom's family's expenses, 47

Groomsmen, 73, 83-84
Guest book and pen, 165
Guests
   average cost of, 46
   inviting, 51-60

Hair, styling, 63, 168
Handkerchief, bridal, 65
Handwritten invitations, 58
Hesitation step, 86-87, 106
Home wedding, 93, 100-101
Homely reception halls, 93-94
Honeymoon, 173-184
"Honeymoon blues," 181
"Honeymoon squeeze," 179
Honeymoon wedding, 34-36
House sitter, 168

Insurance, wedding, 170
Intimate ceremony, 101
Invitations, wedding, 51-60

Jewelry, wedding, 17-23
Jewish wedding, 92, 107

Kneeling pillow, 168

Length
   of engagement, 15
   of honeymoon, 174, 180
Limousine, 159, 162
Lithography, for invitations, 51
Lodging, 164
Luggage, losing, 177-178
Luncheon, bridesmaids', 80

Maid of honor, 29-30
Makeup, 71, 168
Manicurist, hiring, 168

Mantilla veil, 67
Marriage cup, 116
Marriage license, 169
Matron of honor, 29-30
Memorial candle, 104
Menu board, at reception, 131
Military wedding, 101
Mother's gown, wearing, 67
Mother-son dance,
    music for, 156
Mothers' corsages, 152
Mothers' dresses, 86
Music, 153-158

National Limousine
    Association, 162
Nervousness, 69-70, 72, 75, 86-87
Newsletter, wedding, 169-170
Newspaper announcement, 14
Nuremberg Cup, 116

Official, for civil ceremony, 100
Open bar, at reception, 131
"Open church" invitation, 60
Orchestra, for reception, 154

Packing for honeymoon, 180
Parents, 85-87
    divorced, 53, 120, 136
Party
    afterglow, 36, 170
    announcement, 14-15
    bachelor, 73, 77
    engagement, 13-14
Passports, 181-182
Photography/
    videography, 135-146
Planning a wedding, 25-37
Plate service, at reception, 124

Preserving bridal gown, 71-72
Procession, order of, 106-107
Professional Photographers of
    America, 140
Programs, for ceremony, 163
Progressive wedding, 36
Protestant service, 104-106
Pull-away boutonniere, 150

Ranch Vacations, 176
Receiving line, 113-114
Reception, 111-134
    flowers at, 147-152
    music for, 154-158
Reception halls, homely, 93-94
Refreshments, 114-117
Registry
    bridal, 39-43
    gift, 58
    groom, 42-43
Rehearsal, 95-98, 108
Religious ceremony, 28, 99, 101ff
Removable skirt, on gown, 70-71
Reservations, hotel, 178-179
Responses, to invitation, 57-58
Ribbon pull, at reception, 122
Ring
    diamond, 17-20
    engagement, 15, 17-23
    wedding, 19, 21-23
Ring bearer, 19
Romantic honeymoon, 175-176
R.S.V.P., 57

Salon, bridal, 69
Same site wedding, 37
Service, type of, 26-27
Setting, ring, 20
Sheet music for musicians, 167

Shoes, with bridal gown, 67-68
Show, bridal, 70
Shower, wedding, 13
Sites
  ceremony, 99ff
  reception, 112
Size of diamond, 17, 19
Small weddings, 56, 58
Smoke-free reception, 127
Snowball wedding, 79, 86, 90
"Something old, something new," 70
Studio photographer, 137
Surprise wedding, 33

Tails and black top hat, 74
Thank-you notes, 163
Theme, of reception, 126-127
Themes and decorations, 89-94
Thermography, for invitations, 51, 55
Time of wedding, 27
Timetable, reception, 124-126
Tipping, for services, 169, 183
Toasts, 98, 124
Toppers, cake, 128-129
Traditions, at reception, 115
Transportation, 159-162
Travel wedding, 34-36
Traveler's checks, 179
Trends, wedding, 25-26
Tuxedos, 74-76, 83-84
"Two-month" rule, 18-19

Unity candle, 109
Ushers, 73, 84, 108

Veil, bridal, 62-63, 66-67
Victorian theme, 91-92

Videography/ photography, 135-146
Vows, writing your own, 108
Waltz veil, 67
Wedding
  all-night, 36-37
  black and white theme, 90-91
  budget, 49
  cake, 115, 121-122, 129-131
  Christmas, 91
  costume, 37
  dummy cake, 127-128
  favors, 118119
  formal, 74, 113-114
  garden, 93
  gown, 61-71, 80
  home, 93, 100-101
  honeymoon, 34-36
  jewelry, 17-23
  Jewish, 92, 107
  military, 101
  photographer, 137
  progressive, 36
  rings, 19, 21-23
  same site, 37
  small, 56, 58
  snowball, 79, 86, 90
  surprise, 33
  travel, 34-36
  tuxedos, 74-76
  Victorian theme, 91-92
Wedding coordinator, 31-32
Wedding day diaries, 115
Wedding newsletter, 169-170
Weight, losing, 63
White, wearing, 62
"Within the ribbon" seats, 56-57
Wording, for wedding invitations, 52-54, 56